The Path to Your Door

The Path to Your Door

Approaches to Christian Spirituality

Ellen Clark-King

continuum

Continuum International Publishing Group
The Tower Building   80 Maiden Lane
11 York Road   Suite 704
London   New York
SE1 7NX   NY 10038

www.continuumbooks.com

© Ellen Clark-King, 2011

First published 2011

British Library Cataloguing-in-Publication Data
A catalogue record for this book is available from the British Library.

ISBN 978-1-4411-5763-8

Typeset by Fakenham Prepress Solutions, Fakenham, Norfolk NR21 8NN
Printed and bound in India

Contents

Acknowledgements   ix

Introduction   1

1 The Word   9

2 Silence   30

3 Creation and Creativity   49

4 Wilderness   72

5 Body   92

6 Desire   114

7 Mystery   134

Benediction   153

Glossary   156

Suggestions for Further Reading   158

The path to your door
is the path within:
is made by animals,
is lined by flowers,
is lined by thorns,
is stained with wine,
is lit by the lamp of sorrowful dreams:
is washed with joy,
is swept with grief,
is blessed by the lonely traffic of art:
is known by heart:
is known by prayer,
is lost and found,
is always strange,
the path to your door.

Michael Leunig, Common Prayer Collection, *Victoria:*
Collins Dove, 1993.

Acknowledgements

With many thanks to all those who made this book possible – especially Christ Church Cathedral Vancouver for allowing me the time to write and Vaughan Park Retreat Centre Auckland for providing hospitality while I did so.

Introduction

Let me tell you about three well-lived lives, two well known, one not.

The first belongs to an American woman born in 1897 whose early life did not suggest any great spiritual promise. In fact she was defiantly against institutional religion, dropping out of Church and ignoring conventional moral codes: someone who took a teenage sense of rebellion into adulthood. At a time when it was far less acceptable than it is today she was a single parent with failed family relationships. Dorothy Day's unfocused anger and disregard for conventional morality made her an unlikely candidate for sanctity.

What turned her life around was finding in Christ a figure whose love and passion for justice equalled her own and beckoned her to follow. Instead of carrying on a one-woman crusade against conventionality she became part of the Roman Catholic Church and committed to the service of the poor around her. Dorothy never lost her passion and the willingness to challenge accepted customs and authorities, but she gained a new feeling of love, even for those on the other side of the political and social divide: 'We confess to being fools [for Christ], and wish that we were more so … Dear God, please enlarge our hearts to love each other, to love our neighbor, to love our enemy as well as our friend.'[1] Dorothy's conversion to Christianity did not change who she was but it did give her new depth, as well as bringing her new companions in her struggle for justice. She remained – indeed remains – a controversial figure, but she embraced 'Lady Poverty' in as thorough a fashion as St Francis himself – attempting to follow the footsteps of Christ in twentieth-century New York as he had in thirteenth-century Assisi.

Another very different well-lived life began in 354 in Thagaste in Roman North Africa. This was the birth date and place of Augustine of Hippo, one of the most influential theologians of the Western Church. This destiny would have been difficult to predict for those who knew Augustine as a young man. There was, indeed, early evidence of his intense intellectual curiosity and a passionate desire to understand the world through reason. He was never a frivolous person but neither did he find it easy to discover his true calling and path in life. This came about when he was thirty-three years old and finally felt able – even compelled – to make a commitment to the Christianity that he had originally encountered through the faith of his mother.

Augustine was no more perfect than Dorothy. After his conversion experience he continued to be a man who loved argument, who was intellectually arrogant and prone to dismiss other people's points of view, and who occasionally lost sight of divine mercy in his passion for divine justice. But these failings did not stop him being a deeply prayerful person who opened his life to the transformative power of the Holy Trinity. His relationship with God deeply engaged his intellect and motivated him to put his intelligence at the service of the Church. His faith and life do not have the 'touchy-feely' elements that we often associate with spirituality nowadays but it is still apparent that Augustine was a deeply spiritual as well as a deeply intellectual man. His contribution to the life of the Body of Christ may continue to be controversial but it also continues to be rich and fruitful.

My third well-lived life is still being lived as I write. It belongs to someone who would never think of herself as occupying the same category as Dorothy Day, let alone St Augustine. She is someone who will be familiar to readers of my previous book, *Theology by Heart*, and I will continue to use an alias to protect her confidentiality. Enid is a northern English working-class woman who has lived what she would call a very ordinary life, unknown outside her circle of friends and neighbours. She would not think of herself as a spiritual heavyweight, just as a Christian woman trying to live a Christian life to the best of her limited ability. However her life, just like those of Dorothy and Augustine, shows the hallmarks of a genuine Christian spirituality.

Enid lives a life in which her relationship with God colours all her other relationships. She experiences God as accepting love, always warm and welcoming, always concerned for her wellbeing, and for the wellbeing of all His children. And this is how Enid tries to be to those around her. Of course she doesn't always succeed, but her starting point is the living out of the image of God in her everyday life. Those who know her speak of her as a person of compassion and hospitality, and also as someone whose faith is deeply rooted and clearly evident. Nobody would probably call her a saint – it wouldn't be the Geordie way – yet nobody could fail to see the influence that God has in her daily living.

These three very different lives seen together help us understand what Christian spirituality is all about:

1 For each of them spirituality was based on a personal relationship with God ...

2 ... which led them in two directions: on an inward journey and out into greater commitment to the world around them.

3 In Dorothy we see most clearly the commitment to transforming the world for God;

4 in Augustine we see most clearly the synthesis of spirituality and theology;

5 in Enid we see most clearly the possibility of living Christian spirituality in the mundane and everyday circumstances of an 'ordinary' life.

6 For all three Christian spirituality did not only concern their inner wellbeing but was orientated towards others, allowing their neighbours to experience the love and truth of God through their way of living. None of them retreated from the world but none of them looked to the world for ultimate approval of their way of life.

7   All of them made their spiritual journey in companionship with other Christians as part of the Body of Christ.

8   All of them retained their intrinsic personality but all of them also allowed themselves to grow and to change in response to the love of God as they experienced it in their lives.

So, with these three lives before us, let us find a working definition of Christian spirituality that will be the centre from which all our different themes radiate. Christian spirituality is a response – an acceptance of God's invitation to join in the dance of love that is the Trinity. This participation takes us deep within ourselves to where the Holy Spirit breathes through us, and deep into the world where we see the glory of the Creator God revealed and give ourselves in service in companionship with Christ. It is a tuning of our lives to the music of God's truth and love, a singing of God's love song in harmony with all the many other friends of God. Christian spirituality is not a solitary endeavour, nor one whose principal aim is our own wellbeing: it is a journey walked in companionship with fellow followers of Christ in which mutual encouragement and guidance is essential and the end of which is never reached this side of death.

There is another way of putting this in simple words which are, however, no less demanding; a definition of Christian spirituality that is found in the gospels of Matthew, Mark and Luke: 'You shall love the Lord your God with all your heart, and with all your soul, and with all your strength, and with all your mind; and your neighbour as yourself' (Luke 10:27). The twin foci of Christian spirituality are God and our neighbour. It is this outward orientation that sets it apart from most of New Age spirituality which is primarily concerned with the wellbeing of the self. Christian spirituality does also promote self-flourishing, but only as part of a package along with the flourishing of all God's beloved creation – and with a very particular understanding of what it is for the self to truly flourish. Christian flourishing means growing into the likeness of Christ through the work of the Spirit within us as we draw closer into communion with the Source of all being. It is nothing to do with living a socially successful or a stress-free life. It is, however, all to do with living life to the full.

In this book we will explore different ways in which this fullness of life has been experienced. The intention is not to approach spirituality as if we were on an archaeological dig: unearthing interesting fragments from the past in order to examine them dispassionately and gain a greater historical understanding. Instead the intention is to begin a conversation in which our own spiritual experience is in dialogue with the voices of many fellow Christians who have delighted in the spiritual life. In order to ensure that this conversation takes place at more than a merely theoretical level, each chapter will include spiritual exercises which draw on the particular theme being explored. Engaging with these exercises will allow a broader experience of Christian spirituality as well as a broadening of knowledge of spirituality as a subject of study. Each chapter will conclude with a section of Questions for Reflection which invite us to consider some of the theological implications of this strand of the Christian spiritual tapestry.

Academic rigour and spiritual liveliness are excellent companions and flourish in each other's company. Unfortunately they are not frequently found together. There is a strand of spirituality which seems to believe that thought is anathema to true spiritual experience, as well as a strand of academic enquiry which believes that all subjective experience should be banished from serious study. But serious work in spirituality calls for both theory and practice, both thoughtful consideration and heartfelt commitment. Engaging our mind in the study ensures that we don't find ourselves unable to distinguish between the truly spiritual and the merely feel-good. Engaging our heart means that we don't forget that spirituality is about how *we* live *our* life, not just how 'better' Christians than us lived their lives in the past. After all, as was just quoted, you shall love the Lord your God with all your heart and also with all your mind.

We will begin with the place of the word in Christian spirituality, a starting point that allows us to embark on our journey from relatively familiar territory. Although, as will be seen, the seedbed for true spirituality is often believed to be silence, word is actually a crucial component of God's self-revelation and of our reaching out to God in response. So we will see how the Bible informs our spiritual journey, going deep into scripture accompanied by Ignatius of Loyola, and also learning from the riches of the Jesus Prayer tradition. We will then step into silence; a spacious place to explore further. Our two main guides in this area will be Meister Eckhart and Thomas Merton who open up for us some of the spiritual possibilities that lie beyond the grasp of words.

From the richness of silence we will move into the riches of creativity, looking at the spiritual potential in God's creation and in humanity's creative response. We will look for the reality behind the contemporary hype surrounding both Celtic and Franciscan traditions as well as exploring the role of visual and musical art in assisting our spiritual journey. Before we get too comfortable there will be a move to look at the place of wilderness within the Christian tradition; both the literal wilderness of the Desert Fathers and Mothers and the more internal wilderness of the dark night of the soul attested to by John of the Cross. This will include the identification of some of the wildernesses in the world today and how these impact on our spiritual life.

From wilderness we move to a site with a disputed place in Christian spirituality – the body. The chapter will look at dualism, at ascetic spirituality and at the re-evaluation of the body in both Liberation and Feminist spiritualities which make sure that our spiritual thinking remains grounded and incarnational. It will also move from the individual to the corporate by focusing on the Eucharist and our identity as members of the Body of Christ. From the body we move into desire: God's desire for us and the discovery of our own deep desire for God. This is the territory of a number of classic spiritual writers including, in interestingly diverse ways, Ignatius Loyola and Mechthild of Magdeburg. It is also re-imagined in contemporary feminist resources for worship which will also be explored. The final chapter, in a way, brings us back to silence, as it will focus on the continuing mystery of God. However, in exploring the writings of Teresa of Avila, Julian of Norwich and Etty Hillesum we will also find that spirituality and action in the world can never be truly separated. The conclusion is an invitation rather than a summary – an invitation to take your place in the dance of the Triune God that is at the heart of all Christian spirituality, to find your own voice to join in the love-song that the Church has sung to God over many centuries and from many different traditions. It will also suggest the help in our onward journey that a spiritual companion or director can offer.

The nature of this book is to provide a sampler of Christian spirituality, and it is by no stretch of the imagination a comprehensive introduction to all its rich diversity. Some of the choices for inclusion may be idiosyncratic, reflecting what I have found personally helpful on my own spiritual journey. Hopefully it will leave you with a desire to explore further, and with a realization that there is no one right way, but many different right ways, to relate to God in prayer: that there is no one path which leads to God's door, but many paths to choose from.

Note

1. Quoted by Joan Chittister, *A Passion for Life: Fragments of the Face of God*, New York: Orbis Books, 1996, p.61.

Chapter 1

The Word

In the beginning was the Word,
and the Word was with God,
and the Word was God.

John 1:1

We are beginning with word simply because words are what most of us are comfortable with. There are a small number of individuals who instinctively find silence an easy and comfortable space, a slightly greater number who come to appreciate the spacious hospitality of silence through experiencing it in prayer and on retreat, but most of us feel more at home in the world of words and conversation. This, then, needs to be our starting point – because the spiritual journey always begins with where we are and only gently moves us on to where we want, or need, to be. More than this, it is with Word, with God's self-revelation through Jesus Christ and the Holy Spirit, that the whole journey of Christian spirituality began. The whole history of Christian spirituality can be read as our struggle to understand, and fittingly respond, to the Word of God with the help of the indwelling Spirit. Many tools have been discovered and used to make this task easier: human words and human silence both being among them.

The secondary reason to start here is that in today's Church it seems there is often a barrier of suspicion between Christians who emphasize the importance of spirituality and Christians who stress the centrality of the Bible. To put this somewhat crudely: the 'spirituality side' seems to fear that too close attention to the Bible suppresses spirituality in favour of an emphasis on right belief, while the 'Bible side' fears that much spiritual teaching is syncretistic and obscures the simplicity, and uniqueness, of God's revelation in Jesus Christ. This is a mistake on both sides, and a loss to both. In order to try to make this plain our first exploration will be into what the Bible itself teaches us about Christian spirituality. This could be the subject of an entire book in its own right, here we only have space to highlight some of the most important aspects of its teaching.

The Bible and God's relationship with humanity

It is in the Bible that we first learn that God is the creator of humanity and yearns to have a continuing relationship with this creation. In the beginning of Genesis we are told that humanity bears the image of God, but also that this image has been partially obscured through the bad choices that humanity, and individual men and women, have made. The story of the Bible from this point onwards is of God's constant faithful love towards the fallen creation and God's acting to restore the broken relationship and allow the image to regain its intended glory. The initiative within God's relationship with humanity always lies with God: our part is to respond in love, faith and hope to the grace that is constantly offered to us. In other words, the basic premise of the Christian spiritual journey is that God loves us and asks for our love in response, and the basic direction of the Christian spiritual journey is into closer relationship with God.

The Bible tells us some crucial truths about this God who loves us: a revelation which, of course, reached its fullest expression in the life, death and resurrection of Jesus Christ. But even before Jesus' appearance on the scene we have learnt a great deal about God. God is the creator who transcends the whole creation; God is the only source of life and light; God is beyond gender and both women and men bear God's image; God is passionately concerned with the actions and attitudes of humanity; God is infinitely beyond all human imagining and yet closer to human beings than the breath in their own bodies. Any form of Christian spirituality which does not have something of this sense of God as a starting point is likely to end up a long way from the God revealed in the person of Jesus Christ.

It is in Christ that we see most clearly both the nature of God and the human response that is called for from us. In Jesus we see God revealed as self-giving love; a love which offers healing and wholeness of life to those it encounters and which provokes passionate reactions both of devotion and of hostility. In the incarnation God is revealed as willing to accept vulnerability and limitation on our behalf. In the life and ministry of Jesus we see a God who enters fully into the human experience of friendship and celebration as well as of frustration and misunderstanding and pain. In Jesus' betrayal and death we see God's choice to restore the broken relationship with humanity whatever the cost. In Jesus' resurrection is revealed the power of God to defeat death and bring new life to apparently hopeless situations. Finally in Jesus' ascension we see God taking our humanity into the life of the Trinity, welcoming us into the dance of love that is at the heart of God's own being.

The nature of Jesus Christ's birth, life, death, resurrection and ascension are essential to our understanding of the God who calls us into relationship. The way that Jesus lived them out is essential to our understanding of how we are to respond to this call. Jesus' life combined both action and contemplation: as well as teaching and healing we are told that he took time to be alone with God, seeking space to pray away from the noise and demands of his active ministry. In two of these times – the temptations before his ministry began and the agony in Gethsemane near its end – there were particular choices which Jesus made that should resonate for us in our spiritual journeys. In both he seeks out the will of God, taking time to discern the path that God is calling him to take. In the temptations this is both a spiritual and an intellectual exercise as

Jesus rules out possible ways in which God's glory could have been made manifest in order to choose the path of self-giving love. The discernment in Gethsemane has less to do with the mind and more to do with the heart: rather than discerning the right way among many Jesus is discerning whether he can make the choice he knows his Father is asking for – whether his will can be aligned to that of his Father – finally renewing his obedience and trust despite the knowledge of the suffering to come.

God's relationship with us does not end with Jesus: the Bible also teaches us about God's continuing relationship with the world and humanity that is the work of the Holy Spirit. We are not 'left comfortless' after Jesus' ascension but are continually companioned by the Spirit. In fact this is too weak a way of putting it: we are in-dwelt by the Spirit whose presence within us enables our response to God. In other words: it is the Spirit which sanctifies us – working within us to enable us to become more Christ-like or, to use language more familiar to the Eastern than the Western Church, divinizing us. It is in and through the Spirit that Christian spirituality in whatever form is made possible; without the Spirit our human reaching out to the divine would always fail to approach even close to the goal it aimed at.

It would be wrong to think of the Bible as a simple source book for Christian spirituality or as a comprehensive guide to all forms of Christian life. The Spirit has not been idle over the past 2000 years and it would argue an unacceptable degree of stagnation if Christian spirituality had failed to grow and develop in new and exciting ways over that time. But it is also impossible to imagine a vivid and faithful Christian spirituality which did not have the Bible as a core foundation stone. These are the words which provide the starting point for our spiritual journey, and these are the words which frame the silence that the spiritual journey often leads to.

The Lord's Prayer

The place that many of us begin our experience of prayer, and one which we return to again and again wherever that journey takes us within the Christian tradition, is the Lord's Prayer, taught by Jesus to his disciples. Here it is in both its older and newer translations:

Our Father, which art in heaven,	Our Father in heaven,
hallowed be thy name,	hallowed be your name,
thy kingdom come,	your kingdom come,
thy will be done,	your will be done,
on earth as it is in heaven.	on earth as in heaven.
Give us this day our daily bread.	Give us today our daily bread.
And forgive us our trespasses	Forgive us our sins
as we forgive those who trespass against us.	as we forgive those who sin against us.
Lead us not into temptation	Save us from the time of trial
And deliver us from evil. Amen.	and deliver us from evil. Amen

This prayer is the bedrock of our shared experience of Christian praying, one that has been central to both public and private prayer from the Church's earliest days. It is one that we never grow out of but explore again and again for the riches it contains. This section is just a brief reflection on what the Lord's Prayer teaches us about why and how we should pray.

The prayer starts by defining our relationship with God as loving, intimate and familial. It famously does this through Jesus' use of 'abba', father – translated by some commentators as 'daddy', the child's name for their father. This does not mean that we are limited to thinking of God in this one relationship – father to child – but it does mean that we are encouraged to think of God in intimate and personal terms, as one who cares for us and wants to be in relationship with us. Some people are able to see this relationship imaged in that with their own fathers, for others it will come through more clearly in their relationship with their mothers, or others in their lives who have loved them as unconditionally as is humanly possible.

So, in prayer, we approach a God who is in loving relationship with us, and we also approach a God who is 'hallowed' – holy. Rowan Williams explains the importance of this phrase most clearly:

> to ask that God's name be hallowed, that God's name be looked upon as holy, is to ask that in the world people will understand the presence of God among them with awe and reverence, and will not use the name or the idea of God as a kind of weapon to put other people down, or as a sort of magic to make themselves feel safe.[1]

The God we meet in prayer is both loving and intimate and also completely beyond our control – not a God we can manipulate or possess but one who is radically free, bound only by God's own choice of love.

The next phrase is one of the most challenging and far-reaching prayers we can make – that God's kingdom will come. In other words, that this world will be ruled by the divine characteristics of love, peace, joyfulness, generosity, hospitality, gentleness, beauty and forgiveness. We are in effect asking God at this point that we may change – that we may come to embody love, peace, joyfulness, generosity, hospitality, gentleness, beauty and forgiveness. Prayer always has this element to it – that we are to be transformed by it. It is our own personal transformations that are the small starting points for the transformation of the world.

We then ask for our daily bread. Our daily bread – what we need to survive, to go on living. I remember my teenage longing for a part in the school play – at the time I thought that was what I needed to go on living, that that was my daily bread – and promising God that I would never ask for anything else if God would grant this to me (a promise I broke almost immediately!). Such a longing is not quite as ridiculous as it first sounds: as well as bread we do need other things to keep us living: hope, inclusion, love, purpose. All these things are basic human needs which God would have us fulfil for one another. Sometimes we get confused between those things we want and those things we need, but God is much more patient with our human silliness than we are with one another's.

And then comes another reminder that prayer is all about our willingness to change – we pray to be forgiven and to forgive. These two are inextricably linked in a circular movement – we cannot know how to forgive until we know what it is to be forgiven, just as we cannot truly live into our forgiveness unless and until we forgive others. God's forgiveness does not wait on our forgiving others – it always comes first – but its potential to liberate and change us is dependent on our choice to also forgive. In order for our hands to be open to receive God's forgiveness we have to let go of our own hurts and grievances.

The final petition in the Lord's Prayer as recorded by Luke is 'do not bring us to the time of trial' – similar to the phrase the new standard Anglican translation has put in the place of the old 'lead us not into temptation'. It is probable that the 'time of trial' Jesus was thinking of was the apocalyptic end times that figured largely in the theological thinking of his day. However the phrase also has a wider resonance: a plea not to have to confront our own demons until we are ready to do so. It can also be seen as another request to be set free, as Rowan Williams said in the same BBC recording quoted from earlier, this petition asks God to: 'Set us free from all those things, the fears, the sins, the selfish habits that keep us prisoner and that make us unable to face crisis.'

In conclusion there are five truths about prayer that our exploration of the Lord's Prayer reveals. That we pray to a God with whom we are in intimate relationship, but who we do not control. That prayer is about changing ourselves first and foremost so that our world may also be changed. That it is ok to bring our perceived needs to God, knowing that we won't be dismissed or laughed at. That prayer invites us to a place of healing forgiveness for ourselves and for others. That prayer is an appropriate response when we are faced with things that we don't think we can handle. These remain foundational for the Christian understanding of prayer and can provide a path into spiritual maturity just on their own. None of the Christian thinkers and mystics that we will encounter in this book would ever have left this prayer behind even when their own experience took some of them to a place beyond words and images. The Lord's Prayer is one of the essential links between all Christians, and a great gift to all of us who seek to walk the way of Christ.

The psalms in spiritual practice

Many Christians today use the Bible as part of a daily 'quiet time' in which they consciously focus on God, reflect on a scripture passage and spend some time in prayer – often intercession. This mirrors the way that the Bible has been used in Christian worship from earliest days. Listening to, and reflecting on, a reading from the Bible is a foundational Christian practice, one which it inherited from its Jewish roots. In both Jewish and Christian spiritual traditions one of the most frequently used parts of the Bible is the book of Psalms. This is where I will focus, not just because of their centrality to the religious tradition but also because of having seen the impact that their use can have in opening and deepening the prayer lives of individuals.

These 150 poems contain a vast range of human emotion from praise and thanksgiving to complaint and lament and cursing. The experts continue to argue over their original purpose and setting within Jewish worship, but it seems beyond question that the psalms have been used in both public and private devotion from the time they were written. We can infer that they were central to the prayer and worship of Jesus from the way that words from the psalms came to him in his most desolate hour: 'My God, my God, why have you deserted me?' (Psalm 22:1).[2] Their continuing power today is shown in the place they hold in the memories and affections of individuals as they move towards the end of their lives: along with some of the gospel stories it is most often Psalm 23 and Psalm 121 ('I lift up my eyes to the hills') that I have been asked to say with people in pain and at the point of death.

The psalms are marked by great diversity and variety but there is something crucial that unites them. This is more than a particular literary style, or even the fact that they are gathered into one book. The psalms' basic unity lies in the fact that they are all addressing the same divine person; to use the words of one of the foremost scholars of the psalms, Walter Breuggemann, they are addressed to a 'known, named and identifiable You.'[3] In other words they are addressed to a God who is in relationship with the writers and pray-ers of the psalms. A God they know, a God who is intimately concerned with their lives rather than a remote and unmoved deity. And this is perhaps the first lesson of the psalms for all Christian spirituality – that our God is always in relationship with us, always listening, always concerned, always 'you' and never 'it'. There is also a sense of movement through the whole book, despite its diversity. Psalm 1 opens the book with an offering of dutiful obedience, Psalm 150 closes it with an offering of unfettered praise. There is a progression from respectful allegiance to delight in God, including on the way candour and suffering and gratitude: the same movement we look for in our own spiritual lives.

It is possible to divide the psalms into three categories – psalms of the status-quo, psalms of dismay and psalms of new hope – which provides a helpful focus for thinking about their use in personal spirituality.[4] The psalms of status-quo celebrate the world as it is. Into this category fall all the psalms of pure praise and delight, which warmly accept the way things are and speak of a singer contented

with their lot: Psalm 145 for example. These psalms have traditionally provided the Church with words of praise to God, a poetry
of delight and thankfulness for gifts given and graces received. They
can play the same role for us, giving us words when our own voice
falls silent before the bountiful love of God. They do, however, carry
the danger of a certain smugness, of believing ourselves to be in
God's good books while those around us may not be.

So it is when we fall silent from other emotions that the psalms
really come into their own as vehicles for carrying our feelings
to God. It is here where both the other categories – dismay and
new hope – come into play. The psalms of dismay include those
which most offend our contemporary sensibilities and which seem
completely at odds with the Christian imperative of love for God and
neighbour. The prime example of this must be Psalm 58, one which
is usually omitted from public worship because of the virulence of
the curses it contains: 'Let them vanish like water that runs away;
like grass let them be trodden down and wither. Let them be like the
snail that dissolves into slime; like the unseemly birth that never sees
the sun' (Psalm 58:7–8). In all these psalms there is anger, whether at
other people or at God, and a sense that the world is out of step with
the psalmist. These psalms speak with a passionate voice, but one in
which the negative is uttermost.

It might seem that such psalms have no place within Christian
spirituality, which is supposed – at least by those who look in from
the outside – to be a domain of gentleness and light. But Christian
spirituality, if it is to be fully integrated with the rest of life, must be
able to connect with the full range of human emotions: the fear and
anger and frustration as well as the gratitude and love. We often find
it difficult to bring our whole human mess with total honesty to God;
the psalms help us to do so in the knowledge that God's people have
always had to cope with these emotions, and with the assurance that
God will hold us still even when we are hammering our fists against
God's chest.

The psalms help us to base our relationship with God upon an honest recognition of who we are – the dark side as well as the bright. The hope is that we will not stay locked into the world of dismay but may find a path through to the place of new hope, our third category of psalm. These begin in darkness and anguish but end with some resolution of the despair or anger and the sense of a renewed and invigorated trust in God. Psalm 22, which has already been mentioned as the one that Jesus quoted from on the cross, is a prime example of this. It moves from the despair of forsakenness to end with the proclamation of God's deliverance. These psalms, perhaps the largest group numerically, show us something of the benefit of opening our darkest depths to the light of God and the possible transformation that can result. Again the psalms give us words to speak to God when our own words fail: words which have been sanctified by their use across the centuries and across the world. Using the psalms in our spiritual life brings us into contact with the broad stream of Christian experience and unites our prayer with that of the whole community of the Church.

Exercise 1.1: Praying with the psalms

(i)   Find yourself a comfortable position in which you can stay still for a few minutes. This might be sitting cross-legged on the floor, using a prayer stool, or – for most Western people – sitting upright in a chair with both feet resting flat on the floor. It is best to keep the back as straight as possible and to let the hands rest lightly in your lap.

(ii)   Begin your prayer time with a conscious remembrance that you are in God's presence. You may find it helpful to say the Lord's Prayer or 'In the name of the Father, and of the Son, and of the Holy Spirit' or to picture yourself surrounded by a warm presence of unconditional love.

(iii) Read Psalm 139 aloud. Listen to your voice as you speak the words, and listen to your heart and gut to see what feelings they trigger in you.

(iv) Read through the psalm a second time silently, hearing the words as if they were written just for you. Pause with any words or images that catch your attention and again listen for your own emotional response.

(v) Express any thoughts or impressions or intercessions to God.

(vi) End your prayer time with the Gloria, the Lord's Prayer or your own prayer of thanks to God. You might like to write down your feelings in a prayer journal afterwards.

Lectio divina

The psalms, of course are not the only focus of spiritual scriptural reading within the Church. The Benedictine community has given to the wider Church the practice of lectio divina, a particular way of encountering God through the words of the Bible. The lectio divina is a way of gaining extra devotion from the practice of daily Bible reading which has always been a central part of public worship within the Church and especially within the lives of religious communities. It provides a structure for response to the reading, ensuring that the words are heard as resonant for the listener, not only heard by the listener; as Joan Chittister says: 'The Benedictine tradition of lectio, or reflective reading of the sacred books, calls me to take my place among these figures who were called to work out their salvation, as I am, in a world that waits to be reminded by someone of the eternal will of God.'[5]

The basic premise of lectio is that the scripture is living word for us today and not merely a record of the foundation of our faith. So the method of lectio is intended to allow a passage from the Bible to communicate directly to us in a way that brings us a clearer sense of the presence of God in our lives and the life of the world. The method has a four-fold pattern. First you read the word of God – either literally or by calling to mind a particular verse or passage (*lectio*). Rather than concentrating on the whole story you are encouraged to meditate on whatever word or phrase speaks most strongly to you (*meditatio*). This does not mean taking the word as a mantra and using it to empty the mind of other thoughts. It is a more active process than that, involving thinking about the word's meaning, feeling its impact on yourself, building images which lead from the word and even asking questions of God about its implications for your life or for the life of the world. The next stage is the response of prayer to the touch of the word in your heart (*oratio*). This might be thanksgiving or intercession or any other form of honest dialogue with God. The final phase is the passing out from words to the place of silent contemplation when all that is felt is the surrounding presence of God as the rest of the world, even the scripture that began the lectio, is allowed to fall away, its purpose having been fulfilled (*contemplatio*).

The practice of lectio fits well into the Benedictine order of the day, where scripture is regularly read in public worship and where the rule also makes time for 'holy leisure' – under which title lectio divina would come. But it is also a way of prayer that fits well with many contemporary lay Christians understanding of their daily 'quiet time'. Indeed, the many booklets designed to give form to daily prayer and biblical reflection – *Daily Bread* is one example – could be seen as modern day offshoots of the Benedictine tradition. Where they, perhaps, fail to reach as deeply as the classic lectio divina is in stopping short of the final stage of contemplation. They tend to stay within the realm of words rather than reaching out into the realm of silence. And the words they stay with may be those of the writer rather than those of the reader – to put it another way, the reader does not react to the scripture themselves but through the lens of another's interpretation. There is no harm in this, as long as the interpreter is trustworthy, but neither is there as much benefit as allowing the words of the Bible to touch oneself directly and staying with the word or phrase that inspires the greatest reaction in ones own heart.

Exercise 1.2: Lectio divina

(i)   Settle into a physical and mental space of stillness. You might like to use some relaxing music to help you achieve this.

(ii)   Invite the Holy Spirit to be in your mind and heart as you open yourself to scripture.

(iii)   Read John 1:1–14 two or three times, allowing yourself to see which word or phrase stays with you.

(iv)   Reflect on that word or phrase: what it means to you, what it might be telling you, what place it has in your life at this moment.

(v)   Let the word or phrase lead you into prayer. This might be intercession for your needs or for those of others, or thanksgiving, or praise, or penitence.

(vi)   Finally allow the words of your prayer to slip away into silence and experience yourself as being in the presence of the God who gives all words but is beyond all words.

(vii)   When you are ready read the passage a final time as you conclude your prayer.

The Jesus Prayer

The next form of prayer continues the theme of words, although this time they are not directly biblical and are used in a very different way. The Jesus Prayer today usually consists of the words 'Lord Jesus Christ, Son of God, have mercy on me, a sinner.' The words echo those of the publican in Luke 18:13, whose humility won him justification; and those of the blind beggar in Luke 18:38, who calls out for Jesus' help. It is the classic prayer of the Eastern Church although it has also found many practitioners within the contemporary West. This is not surprising as it is such a simple form of prayer to use and one, as will be seen, that can fit into the small gaps of a busy modern life.

The origins of the Jesus Prayer lie in the practices of the fourth-century Desert Fathers and Mothers, who advocated the use of a short phrase to keep the mind focused on prayer. However there is no evidence at this time for the use of the words of the Jesus Prayer itself. This is first recorded in the sixth century, although without the phrase 'Son of God'. However it is really from the fourteenth century on that its use became widespread within the Orthodox Churches, and especially in the monastic life of Mt Athos. At this time the saying of the prayer became associated with a particular posture and pattern of breathing: the pray-er was to sit with bowed head, the eyes fixed on the place of the heart, slowly repeating the first phrase of the prayer with the inward breath and the second half with the outward breath. The intention of this posture was to help the pray-er descend from the realm of the mind and intellect to that of the heart. At this period the term 'hesychasm', which is derived from the Greek for 'stillness' or 'quiet', came to be associated with the Jesus Prayer.

It was in the eighteenth century that the Jesus Prayer began to make a real impact on Orthodox spirituality outside the monasteries. This was the result of a work called the *Philokalia*, edited by St Nicodemus of the Holy Mountain, which gathered together writings about the Orthodox spiritual way, and especially the Jesus Prayer. Another very influential work, published in nineteenth-century Russia and still popular today, is the anonymous *Way of the Pilgrim*,[6] which tells the story of a nameless wanderer, crossing Russia with only his Bible, a backpack and some bread, and trying to live out the command to 'pray without ceasing'. This work, perhaps more effectively than any other, made the Jesus Prayer accessible to lay Christians; among whom its use continues to flourish in the West now as well as in the East.

This brief history of the prayer may give it a sense of context, but it does little to show why so many Christians value it so highly. In order to explore this it is helpful to look at two of the ways that the Prayer is used today. The first of these is repetition, whether by an individual or by a group. The words of the prayer are said over and over so that there is no room in the consciousness for anything else but the awareness of God. A frequently used aid for this way of prayer is a prayer-rope. This is usually less elaborate than a rosary, consisting of a rope with, usually a hundred, knots – each knot marking a repetition of the prayer. This rope provides a tactile accompaniment to the prayer, again helping the pray-er to stay focused. The point of this repetition is to keep the pray-er consciously in the presence of God. Other words and thoughts drop away leaving an inner silence underneath the repetition: a silence which is open to, and receptive of, the Spirit of God.

There is a second way of using the Jesus Prayer that many people find valuable today. That is to say the prayer whenever is possible in the gaps between the busyness of their lives. So, for example, one might say it in the car when driving to work, or at the sink while washing up, or in the few moments' breathing space between teaching lessons. The brevity and simplicity of the prayer lends itself well to this practice and, as with the more formal repetition, it is a way of reminding oneself of the presence of God with us at all times. It allows the pray-er to consciously make the connection with God whatever the distractions and demands of everyday life. I have found it a prayer that fits in perfectly with a bus commute into work.

In whatever way the Jesus Prayer is prayed its words express something fundamental to the Christian understanding of spirituality. It begins by calling on the name of Jesus Christ and naming him as Lord. It continues by identifying Jesus as Son of God, thus reminding us of the relationships that are at the heart of the Trinity. The second half of the prayer contains a plea for forgiveness and transformation: the work of the Holy Spirit in the world. The last words of the prayer are probably the most controversial, and perhaps the least necessary. Naming yourself a sinner is, for many, a helpful reminder of our connection with the whole of sinful humanity and an aid to humility. For others, however, it is an unhelpful addition which acts only to remind them of their inadequacy and may even make them question the possibility of God's love and forgiveness. It is quite possible to say the Jesus Prayer authentically without these last words or, as many do, to replace the term 'a sinner' with the name of a person or cause that you wish to intercede for. In whatever way it is prayed, saying the Jesus Prayer unites the pray-er with a whole host of Christians across the world who find these words bring them to a closer sense of the presence and the love of God.

Exercise 1.3: The Jesus Prayer

Steps i and ii as before.

(iii)   Become aware of all the different sounds you can hear, not trying to analyse them but just being aware of them. Focus first on the sounds from outside the room, then on any inside the room, and finally on the sounds of your own body, especially your breathing. Either shut your eyes or leave them slightly open and unfocused.

(iv)   When you feel settled and still begin to recite the Jesus Prayer, using either the form 'Lord Jesus Christ, Son of God, have mercy on me, a sinner' or 'Lord Jesus Christ, Son of God, have mercy on me'. Whenever you find your thoughts wandering, as they are bound to do, gently bring your attention back to the words of the prayer.

(v)   You might want to set a time limit for this prayer. The simplest way to do this is to set an alarm clock so that you aren't constantly tempted to check the time. Alternatively you might want to decide how many repetitions you will say and use a knotted string, or beads, to keep count with your fingers.

(vi)   If you wish to include some intercessions in this prayer time then for some time say the prayer as 'Lord Jesus Christ, Son of God, have mercy on N.'

(vii)   Bring your prayer time to an end by saying the Gloria, the Lord's Prayer or your own prayer of thanks to God. Again you might like to write down any experiences and reactions to this prayer in a prayer journal.

Kataphatic spirituality

I want to end this chapter with a brief look at the stream of Christian
spirituality which welcomes an abundance of words and images
as part of the human response to God's self-revelation. This broad
tradition is known as kataphatic – embracing imagery and words
as a way to grow in understanding of God. At the other end of the
spectrum, which we will come to later in the book, is apophatic
spirituality, where all words and images are abandoned as unable to
bring one close to the heart of the mystery of God. This is not to say
that kataphatic spirituality believes that God is contained or compre-
hended within our human understanding, but rather that a plethora
of words and images is one of the best ways that we have been given
for getting closer to a sense of who God is, and what God calls us to
grow towards.

It would be wrong to say that kataphatic spirituality welcomes all
words and images as having something to tell us of the truth of who
God is. The language and pictures we use must have a starting point
in God's self-revelation in Jesus Christ so, while no term reaches
close to the divine reality, it is still appropriate to talk of God as
love and inappropriate to talk of God as hate. However, kataphatic
spirituality is the spirituality that likes to say 'yes'. 'Yes, God is love.'
'Yes, God is truth.' 'Yes, God is revealed in the beauty of creation.'
'Yes, God is Father.' 'Yes, God is Trinity.' 'Yes, God is mystery beyond
imagining and far beyond the limited grasp of human understanding.' It is a spirituality of affirmation as opposed to a spirituality
of negation: knowing God to be beyond all human concepts it feels
free to explore a whole range of images and words none of which
capture the divine essence but all of which illuminate some tiny part
of that essence. The fact that our language always fails to describe
God gives a freedom to explore a superabundance of words, always
keeping in mind that God is none of them yet may be hinted at by
all of them.

It might be fair to say that the focus in kataphatic spirituality is more on our relationship with God than on the inner reality of Godself. We find a wealth of words to describe *who God is for us* – how we are called to relate to God – rather than ever finding words which are adequate for expressing truly *who God is*. In the same way that we seek to deepen our personal relationships by learning more about each other, so kataphatic prayer calls us to communicate with God and so deepen this relationship through conversation and mutuality. After all, language remains our primary vehicle of communication however inadequate it may ultimately be.

Kataphatic prayer invites us on a voyage of discovery as we explore new ways of speaking to and of God. It is one of the most exciting truths about our Christian spiritual journey that there is always more to find out about God: we never reach the end of the divine infinity. Words may not take us the whole way on this journey of exploration but, without them, we would not know that we needed to start or which direction to follow. I do not subscribe to the idea that there is a hierarchy of Christian spiritual practice: that silence and apophatic spirituality is superior to words and kataphatic spirituality. All of these are only tools given by God to help us on our way, and different people will find different ones more or less helpful. The end is never finding the right words, or immersing ourselves in the most complete silence; the end is always God.

Exercise 1.4: Exploring your names for God

Kataphatic spirituality invites us to discover our own names for God – this prayer exercise is a way of doing that.

Steps i and ii as before.

(iii)   Read Isaiah 43:1–7 through slowly at least twice. Try and hear God's words of love as spoken directly to you.

(iv)   Put the Bible aside and close your eyes.

(v)   Let yourself think of all the names that God has for you. Imagine God calling you by your given name and by your nickname if you have one. Then imagine some of the other names God has for you – 'daughter', 'son', 'child', 'disciple', 'seeker', 'beloved', 'servant', 'friend' – or any others.

(vi)   Then let yourself think of the names that you have for God. These might be biblical – 'Rock', 'King', 'Father', 'Lord', 'Saviour' – or they might be personal from your own experience of God – 'Mother', 'Beloved', 'Absent One', 'Light'.

(vii)   Spend as long as you need considering these names, perhaps focusing on one and allowing the image of it to fill your mind.

(vii)   Read Isaiah 43:1–7 again using your name for God and God's name for you.

(viii) End with the Gloria or the Lord's Prayer or your own prayer of thanks. Consider writing your impressions in a prayer journal.

Questions for further reflection

(1)   There are many different ways within Christianity of interpreting the Bible, and different emphases placed on the importance of the scripture to our contemporary spiritual life. Some Christians feel that any spiritual practice needs to be justified by reference to the Bible's teaching on prayer, while others would say that the traditions of the Church and the positive experience of other Christians is validation enough. Where do you fall on this spectrum?

(2)   This second question is related to the first, but slightly different. How important is the Bible for your spiritual life? Is it something that you use regularly as a source of spiritual insight – whether through a practice like lectio divina or through regular Bible reading – or is your spiritual life completely separate from your relationship with the Bible? Can you articulate theological reasons for your choice, and are you aware of any theological consequences?

(3)   The Lord's Prayer is a foundational text for prayer within the life of the Church. Are you comfortable with modern revisions to

the prayer which change terms such as 'our father' to 'our father/ mother' or do you believe these alter its fundamental meaning?

Notes

1. From *Reflections on the Lords Prayer*, recorded for the BBC in August 2009.
2. There is continued debate over whether this should be seen as a cry of total desolation, or a cry of desperate hope as Psalm 22 goes on to speak of the vindication and deliverance of the one who is suffering.
3. *The Psalms and the Life of Faith*, ed. Patrick D. Miller, Minneapolis: Fortress Press, 1995, p.34.
4. These three categories are loosely based on the three-fold division of psalms into orientation, disorientation and reorientation used by Breuggemann, although my division has more to do with the practicalities of spirituality than scholarly research. Breuggemann's categories are defined in Chapter 1 of *The Psalms and the Life of Faith*, ed. Patrick D. Miller, Minneapolis: Fortress Press, 1995.
5. Joan Chittister OSB, *Wisdom Distilled from the Daily: Living the Rule of St Benedict Today*, San Francisco: Harper and Row, 1990, p.34.
6. *The Way of a Pilgrim and the Pilgrim Continues His Way*, tr. R. M. French, New York: HarperOne, 1991.

Chapter 2

Silence

Be still, and know that I am God.

Psalm 46:10

We live in a world that works as hard as it can to banish silence from our everyday experience. This is true, at least, in the urbanized and industrialized societies of the more affluent third of the world. We have even invented a sub-music – popularly known by its most famous trademark, muzak – in order to cover awkward silences in elevators, and insist on playing tinny versions of popular classics when leaving callers waiting on the phone. Silence is the enemy of ease: it is seen as a failure in communication, an awkward pause between the business of talk, rather than as something which is good and valuable in its own right.

But many people are finding a hunger for silence despite its poor reputation: a need to step away from the noise and busyness of modern life and rediscover the potential of quiet and rest. You only have to look at the burgeoning retreat industry to see that this is the case. There is a realization that in losing silence we have lost something of great value both for our spiritual journey and for our psychological wellbeing. We human beings need down-times when we are not being bombarded with stimuli or being required to react to a dozen different information in-puts at once. Multi-tasking may be a useful life skill but it is also a tiring way to live, and one which inevitably contributes to our characteristic modern ailments of stress and burn-out.

So what is it about silence that both attracts and repels us? My guess would be that it is the emptiness of it. Silence takes away our distractions and leaves us with our selves and, of course, with God. It also takes away the demand that we constantly interact with others and strive to meet their expectations of us. In silence there is nothing to focus on outside of our selves; no hiding place of chatter for us to lose ourselves in. It is a space where we are forced to become aware of what is going on inside us, and this can often be an uncomfortable experience. In other words, silence, though we may think of it as the opposite of communication, is actually a place of encounter. And encounter of the most intimate kind: with our inner truths and with our God.

It is not, therefore, surprising that silence is seen as a primary tool for working at our spiritual lives. Silence allows us to take stock of the reality of ourselves and of our relationship with God; it also gives us the chance to catch the still small whisper of God's voice calling to us. Silence also reminds us that the initiative in our spiritual journey does not lie with us but with God. We are meant to listen and respond rather than to dictate and command. Entering into silence is a way for us to enter into this responsive space and to allow the agency and control of our lives to shift from our hands to God's. The shape of this silence is framed not by the command 'shut up' but by the invitation to sit quietly and comfortably with the one who knows us best. What we hear in this space may be challenging as well as comforting but its purpose is to help us to know God, and ourselves, better.

The Cloud of Unknowing

Entering into this nurturing silence is not as easy as simply ceasing to talk. That may be a necessary first step but it doesn't take us far enough. For the vast majority of us, such external silence only makes us more aware of all the noise and chatter that is going on inside our own head. It is achieving silence on the inside that is the real accomplishment, and something that has been the goal of various forms of prayer and meditation, both within the Christian spiritual community and in other spiritual paths. Indeed when considering silence as prayer many people's first thought is of the Eastern, especially the Buddhist, tradition rather than the Christian. Buddhism is seen as the natural home of contemplation while Christian prayer is believed by many to focus almost exclusively on intercession, confession and praise – all three very wordy ways of praying.

However this is to ignore a crucial – and central – component of the Christian spiritual path. Christian prayer has never been only understood as our taking time to communicate with God through words that arise from our heart, or through words that are set down for public and corporate use. This is, indeed, a part of prayer for the vast majority of Christians but not its entirety. Prayer has always also meant an opening up of ourselves to God, attending to God, resting in God's presence and allowing God to be with us. And it is these forms of prayer which lead us into the realms of meditation and contemplation and which require a silencing of our inner voice as well as of our outer one.

One of the most famous spiritual classics that invites its readers into this silence is the fourteenth-century writing *The Cloud of Unknowing*. It was published anonymously, as is perhaps appropriate for a writer who emphasizes humility so greatly. We know that the writer was English, probably from the Midlands by the dialect in which he writes, and a contemplative monk. There is little else known about him for certain, although most experts believe the author was a member of the Carthusian order which encouraged the eremetical style of living that *The Cloud* praises. The author might have been a priest, a theory suggested by the blessing that he includes at the end of the book. However such speculation is unimportant for most readers of *The Cloud* whose focus is less on its origins and more on its potential relevance for their own spiritual journey.

The period when it was written was one of great social change and unrest as society struggled to come to terms with the immense human disaster of the Black Death. It was no easier for men and women then to step away from the press of concerns and the demands of daily living in order to find space for inner silence than it is for us today. Indeed, the author of *The Cloud* thought that this was a calling for only a very small and select number of people, those who have achieved the highest level of Christian life. Most people remain at the 'ordinary' level, where they are able to achieve salvation but not to move beyond a life absorbed in daily practical concerns. Some are called to the 'special' walk of life where they are able to add some degree of contemplation to their activity, usually through entering a religious order. The third degree are those called to the 'singular' level which, for the author, means those who follow the hermit's vocation. Finally there are a very few called to be 'perfect' who, through following the exercise of prayer that the author teaches, are able to achieve some fleeting moments of union with God in this life. This hierarchical schema does not sit well with our contemporary sensibilities and, as will be seen in the next section, this prayer is now being taught as a way that anyone can utilize.

It is true that the way of prayer of *The Cloud of Unknowing* can seem fairly daunting on first acquaintance:

> For when you first begin to undertake it, all that you find is a darkness, a sort of cloud of unknowing; you cannot tell what it is except that you experience in your will a simple reaching out to God.[1]

This cloud and darkness is caused by our inability to understand God through the power of our intellect. Our reason is too feeble to comprehend who God is and we need, instead, to rely on what *The Cloud* calls our 'loving power' to bring us closer to God. The cloud of unknowing that separates us from God can never be penetrated by the work of the mind but only by 'a sharp dart of longing love'; as *The Cloud* says: 'By love he [God] may be grasped and held; by thought never.' The author is also very clear that all we need to do in prayer is hold ourselves open to God, it is God who does the rest:

> He [God] asks no help, but only you yourself. His will is that you should simply gaze at him and leave him to act alone. Your part is to keep the windows and the doors against the inroads of flies and enemies ... Call upon him then, and let us see how you get on. He is always most willing, and is only waiting for you.[2]

Our best approach to prayer, therefore, is to put our thinking to one side and simply allow ourselves to be in the presence of God. The author spends some time explaining a method that makes this form of prayer possible, along with pointing out various problems and distractions that the novice pray-er is likely to encounter – the 'flies' and 'enemies' mentioned above. The central approach involves treading down any thoughts that arise, however good and holy in themselves, so that you can be more completely open to God. All thoughts, not just negative or frivolous ones, get between you and God because they are simply not capable of reaching the transcendence that is God. In order to accomplish this absence of thought which, for most of us, is extremely difficult, the author suggests that the pray-er should focus on a single, short word – 'God' and 'love' are two that he suggests. He uses the imagery of a spear and a shield for this word: it can be used to see off any thoughts that arise during the prayer, though it is not intended to be the focus of the prayer or used as a mantra. The aim is silence of the mind, the word is only used when that silence has been interrupted.

The point and purpose of this prayer is to enable you to 'offer yourself to God, the whole of you as you are, to all of him as he is.' It is a prayer of passivity rather than activity: the activity lies with God while our part is just to open ourselves up to God and keep down any barriers that might arise. It is also a prayer of the heart rather than the mind because, as the author of *The Cloud* puts it, 'a soul is wherever it loves'.

Centering prayer

A contemporary interpretation of *The Cloud*'s way of prayer can be found in centering prayer. This form of prayer is particularly identified with the Cistercian Father Thomas Keating who has championed it as a contemporary spiritual practice. Like the author of *The Cloud of Unknowing*, Fr Keating does not suggest that this is a way of prayer that will work for all Christians; although he would be less forthright than *The Cloud* about suggesting that it was superior to all other forms of prayer. Instead, Keating and others talk about those who have a special calling to this form of contemplative prayer for whom more wordy forms feel increasingly inadequate. These are not people whose spirituality is at a higher level than other, less advanced, individuals but merely those who have a particular spiritual hunger which only this particular way of prayer will feed.

However, having said that, there are proponents of this form of prayer who would see it, as the author of *The Cloud* does, as the pinnacle of all spiritual experience: Cynthia Bourgeault, another well-known contemporary advocate of centering prayer, has certainly spoken of it in this way. In my opinion this is not helpful. No spiritual path, however helpful or advanced, is an end in itself: the end is always a closer relationship with God and a greater desire to serve our neighbour. For some people this will certainly be facilitated by centering prayer but for others this way of prayer will not be helpful – and that does not mean that they are failing to make the grade spiritually. It is a great gift that this form of prayer has returned to popular awareness within the Church, but it will militate against its usefulness if it comes to be seen as the only 'advanced' way of prayer. Better for it to be known as a richly rewarding path for those called to it rather than as the only path towards true Christian maturity.

Like the prayer of *The Cloud*, centering prayer is a passive rather than active way of praying: a form of prayer characterized by surrender. It is an intentional way into silence in which we willingly let go of all the distractions and preoccupations which usually occupy our attention. Entering into this silence is also seen as a way to get behind the 'false selves' that our ego-driven words construct and into our truest self where we are most receptive to God's Spirit. Silence is not so much an end in itself as a way for us to be most truly ourselves with God – as open to God's grace as we can allow ourselves to be.

The method suggested for achieving this mirrors very closely that of *The Cloud*. The pray-er begins with the intention to be as open to God as possible and to consent to the action of God's grace; expecting, like the author of *The Cloud*, that God is always waiting and eager to be invited in. During the time of prayer all that the pray-er does is to keep silence as far as is possible, surrendering every thought as soon as it occurs without paying any attention to it whatsoever. A tool for keeping the attention away from the thoughts that always occur is a short word chosen by the pray-er in advance. Each time the pray-er refuses to focus on a thought that occurs is understood as a surrender to God – a willing putting aside of one's own affairs in order to be open to God's affairs. This means that a prayer time which is full of thoughts is considered as beneficial as one in which the talking mind is completely silenced and at rest: it is not the felt result that is important but the attitude of openness to God that offers the potential for gracious transformation.

Centering prayer thus far follows very closely the shape of prayer within *The Cloud*. Its modern practitioners have, however, also developed it in a direction that is more responsive to our cluttered contemporary lives; providing a form of prayer that can become a habitual part of our response to everyday events, especially those which stress or distress us. The first step is to open yourself, and especially your body, to whatever it is that you are experiencing. Not analysing the experience but allowing yourself to feel how it is being lived out in your body. The second step, and the most counter-intuitive, is to welcome the feeling whatever it may be, consciously saying to oneself, 'welcome fear, anger, unhappiness'. The intention of this is to accept those parts of ourselves and our feelings that we more usually try to hide and repress, therefore allowing us to be more in touch with who we are and to have no parts of ourselves that are not open to God's grace. The third step is to let go of the situation and experience; to stop trying to control it and leave it for God to take care of. The key to this last part is a habit of mind that reminds us that we are always safe within the presence of God and that nothing which happens to us is bad enough to change that fact. With these three steps our experience is brought into our relationship with God and consecrated through our realization of God's presence with us in the midst of it. We entrust all of our self to God.

Exercise 2.1: Into the cloud

(i)   Find yourself a place and a time when you can hope to be undisturbed.

(ii) Before you begin your prayer set a quiet and unobtrusive alarm clock so that you don't have to worry about timing yourself. About twenty minutes is a recommended amount of time for this type of prayer.

(iii) Choose a word that you will use as a returning point whenever you become aware that you are thinking. This should ideally be short and not something that you will be tempted to dwell on and analyse. Suggestions include: 'God', 'Peace', 'Let go', 'Love', 'Hope', 'Still', 'Joy'.

(iv) State, either silently or out loud, your intention to be fully open to God's presence and to surrender all your self to God.

(v)   Begin by repeating your word to yourself until you can feel the chatter of your mind beginning to drop away.

(vi) Stay with the inner silence as long as it is present, returning to your word again whenever thoughts intrude.

(vii) Do not be surprised, or feel you have failed, if your entire twenty minutes is spent without any inner quiet. Just continue to surrender to God's presence, refusing to follow a thought when you become aware of it, and gently returning to your word.

(viii) At the end of your time of prayer, give thanks to God and invite God's continued presence with you as you return to the business of your day.

Meister Eckhart

With Meister Eckhart the journey into silence takes on another dimension. Rather than the focus being on our own inner silence it shifts to a necessary silence about God's self. Eckhart is one of the best known proponents of what is called 'apophatic theology' or the 'way of unknowing'. In our last chapter we encountered the opposite of this in kataphatic theology and spirituality: the way to God as paved with a superabundance of images and metaphors. The apophatic way, on the contrary, is stripped bare of all words and images as no human construct can come close to capturing even a small part of the essence of who God is. If we try to come to God through words we only arrive at an idol of our own making and end up masking the true God with our inadequate imaginings. The only path that leads us truly towards God is (somewhat confusingly!) no path at all – only when we stop being concerned with ways and words will we be truly capable of drawing close to the divine reality.

It is not surprising that Meister Eckhart's thought was controversial and not easily accepted by the Church hierarchy. He was born in about the year 1260 in the Germanic region of Thuringia and became a Dominican studying in both Cologne and Paris. His thoughts have come down to us in two main sources: his sermons which were preached and written in German and his Latin writings. During his lifetime he was suspected of heresy, and Pope John XXII in a Papal Bull of 1329 declares certain of Eckhart's statements heretical. Before this event Eckhart had already made a statement saying that his interest was only in the truth and that he willingly retracted anything in his teaching that the Church deemed to be false. It is probable that his death occurred between this statement and the issuing of the Bull. It is also probable that the decision of the general chapter of the Dominicans at Toulouse in 1328 to proceed against preachers who 'endeavour to preach subtle things which not only do (not) advance morals, but easily lead the people into error' was aimed at both Eckhart and his followers.

It is undoubtedly true that Eckhart's theology is difficult to follow, not just because his philosophical background was very different from our own, but also because his body of work, which includes Latin commentaries written for the academy and German sermons preached for the people, sometimes appears self-contradictory. However, there are two fundamental parts of Eckhart's understanding which do speak specifically to the place of silence in Christian spiritual practice. The first is his understanding that God is beyond all our attempts to name the divine reality, and the second is his repeated teaching that those who seek a 'way of prayer' end up finding a way but missing God.

Eckhart's apophatic understanding is that all names not only fall short of the divine reality but also create a barrier between ourselves and God: putting something that is not God in the place of God. He even wanted to get behind the Trinitarian images of God to the 'hidden God', the 'Absolute Existence' that is his most frequently used name for the deepest reality of God. This God beyond all names calls us into silence: 'The most beautiful thing which a person can say about God would be for that person to remain silent from the wisdom of an inner wealth. So, be silent and quit flapping your gums about God.'[3] But more fundamentally than this, the God without names calls us into union with himself, into the place of oneness where all being has its source and finds its true resolution in return.

Some of Eckhart's strongest language is reserved for those who think that they, and everyone else, can achieve this reunion by following a particular spiritual path or set of religious practices. He doesn't mince his words: 'To all outward appearances persons who continue properly in their pious practices are holy. Inwardly, however, they are asses. For they know about God but do not know

God.'[4] Our spiritual calling is not to fill ourselves up with spiritual practices but to empty ourselves out so that we can be filled with God. One of Eckhart's controversial, and beautiful, ideas was that the Son is born within each individual soul, God's grace working within us to bring Godself to birth in our human lives.

There is one attitude that Eckhart does encourage in his listeners, and that is detachment. By which Eckhart means that we need to empty ourselves of the things which would fill us up and leave no room for God: not primarily possessions and attachments but the interior attitudes and desires which get in the way of allowing God to be God. In this category would come forms of prayer which focus on asking God for benefits, rather than on asking God for God; and any attachment to a way of prayer which becomes an end in itself: 'Whoever is seeking God by ways is finding ways and losing God, who in ways is hidden.'[5] Our path to reunion with God lies not in finding a path to walk on ourselves but in allowing ourselves to be open and empty so that God may be born in us.

Exercise 2.2: The way of no names

(i)   Find a comfortable position for prayer and spend a few minutes settling into the silence.

(ii)   Bring to mind some of the names for God that you had as a child. These could be biblical or from another religious tradition or from your own experience. The name could even be 'the one who does not exist'.

(iii)   Dwell with each name for a few moments, and then put each one aside. You might want to say to yourself, 'God is more than I can name', as you do this.

(iv)   Now bring to mind some of the names you have for God now. This may be a similar list or a completely different one.

(v)   Again dwell with each name for a few moments, and then put each one aside, using the same phrase if you find it helpful.

(vi)   Spend time with these words of Eckhart's: 'God does not ask

anything else of you except that you let yourself go and let God
be God in you.'

(vii)   Conclude your prayer time by thanking God for all the ways
in which God comes to you and for all the times that you have
been able to be open to receive God; remembering, as Eckhart
said, that 'If the only prayer you said in your entire life is thank
you, it will be enough.'

Thomas Merton

One of the most revered writers of the twentieth century about the
way of prayer, and the place of silence within spirituality, was the
American monk Thomas Merton. His childhood was not an easy
one: he was born in France on 31 January 1915 to two artists: an
American mother and a New Zealander father. His mother died
when he was only 6 and his father when he was 16. His first book,
the autobiography *The Seven Storey Mountain*[6] which was published
in 1948, shows him as a dissatisfied and rootless young man until
his conversion to Roman Catholicism at the age of 23. Three years
after this, in 1941, he entered the Trappist Abbey of Our Lady of
Gethsemani in Kentucky. This was his home for the rest of his life,
although his vocation as a teacher of contemplation and as an activist
for social change meant that he also travelled more than was usual
for a Trappist monk. Merton died on 10 December 1968 when he
was electrocuted by a faulty lamp while attending a conference on the
future of monasticism in Bangkok. By the time of his death he was
probably the best-known monk in the Western world.

I first encountered Merton through the pages of *The Seven Storey
Mountain*, which was probably a mistake. He comes across as
passionate and committed to God in this book but also as bigoted
and somewhat arrogant. Merton recognized this himself, as his
friend and biographer Jim Forest tells us: 'Later in life Merton was
dismayed at how narrow and judgmental he had been and claimed
that the author of *The Seven Storey Mountain* was dead and buried.'[7]

Part of Merton's change of heart is attributable to an experience that he famously had in 1958, an experience which warmed his previously cool attitude to his fellow human beings as he found a new sense of connection and communion with 'ordinary' men and women:

> In Louisville, on the corner of Fourth and Walnut, in the center of the shopping district, I was suddenly overwhelmed with the realization that I loved all those people, that they were mine and I theirs, that we could not be alien to one another even though we were total strangers. It was like waking from a dream of separateness, of spurious self-isolation in a special world, the world of renunciation and supposed holiness.[8]

Merton had by no means lost his sense of vocation but he was opening up to an understanding of spirituality which was focused more on the benefit to others than to his own search for holiness: a change which became visible in his increasing involvement with the peace and social rights movements of the 1960s.

While Merton's focus was turning outwards, he was also looking for more physical isolation. His Trappist community was a crowded building in which the monks lived in dormitories and which, while promoting silence, did not allow for much personal privacy. Merton felt a constant calling towards a way of life that would allow for more time alone, and pushed to be allowed to live in a hermitage within the Abbey grounds. This was finally granted to him, and he found it both met a deep need but also was a constant challenge: 'It is a full time job coping with one's own damn mind in solitude.'[9] Not that Merton's solitude was ever complete. He continued to correspond with a wide range of people, from activists like Dorothy Day to Muslim and Buddhist scholars, and to have guests at the hermitage. He even fell in love in 1966 – with Margie, a nurse at the Louisville hospital where he had an operation on his back. He struggled to remain committed to his monastic vocation while also feeling a calling to marriage and the intimacy of romantic, sexual love. Merton's journey through life was never simple or straightforward but instead reflected his complex character and the way that he wanted to throw himself whole-heartedly in so many different directions – all of which could be ways of living out the love of God for the world.

One of the other constant paradoxes of Merton's life was that his desire to communicate ran parallel with his desire to find a place of deep silence. It is somewhat ironic to read these words from his journals, remembering that he was the author of thirty-five books, as well as his journals and numerous letters: 'in my prayer and all my interior life, such as it is, I am concerned with the need for a greater and more complete interior silence: an interior secrecy that amounts to not even thinking about myself. Silence about my prayer, about the development of my interior life, is becoming an absolute necessity.'[10] It is true that Merton focused on talking about prayer, more especially contemplation, in general terms rather than drawing explicitly on his own experience. One of the few places where he described his own way of prayer is in a letter to a Muslim scholar, Abdul Aziz, in 1966 as 'a kind of praise rising up out of the Center of Nothing and Silence.' But perhaps his most vivid words on the subject are these lines from *Thoughts in Solitude*: 'My life is a listening. His [God's] is a speaking. My salvation is to hear and respond. For this, my life must be silent. Hence, my silence is my salvation.'[11]

Merton did not only value silence for his own prayer life but saw it as an essential part in any Christian's ability to move towards contemplation. By 'contemplation' Merton means that place in prayer where there is complete openness to God; a place where all the false selves of a person fall away and die leaving only the true self alive in Christ. He realizes that not all Christians are called to this form of prayer, which is one that takes great commitment from the pray-er and yet is always, finally, a pure gift from God which we can never achieve by our efforts alone. However he does believe that all Christians need places and times of silence in order to get in tune with God. This is expressed beautifully in a passage from *New Seeds of Contemplation*:

Let there always be quiet, dark churches in which men can take refuge. Places where they can kneel in silence. Houses of God, filled with His silent presence. There, even when they do not know how to pray, at least they can be still and breathe easily. Let there be a place somewhere in which you can breathe naturally, quietly, and not have to take your breath in continuous short gasps. A place where your mind can be idle, and forget its concerns, descend into silence, and worship the Father in secret.[12]

Merton saw silence and prayer as a place where human beings could discover their true selves, the self that was given them by God and which reflects God's love to the world. Noise constricts lives, while silence allows a deeper breath and a deeper understanding. Silence is a more natural, and more healthy, milieu for people than the noise with which we are usually surrounded because it is a better environment for encountering both God and our true identity. Families were urged by Merton to silence their radios and TVs so that they could hear the truth of reality beyond the distraction of constant chatter and so find both God and themselves.

In exploring silence and contemplation Merton encountered the spiritual traditions of Asia, and found especial value in his engagement with Zen. Zen, for Merton, was not to be identified with any particular religious system – it was not identical with Buddhism. Instead he saw Zen as a trans-religious consciousness, a way of pointing to the wordless experience that comes before any religious systematization or doctrine. As he says in his book *Zen and the Birds of Appetite*: 'the chief characteristic of Zen is that it rejects all these systematic elaborations in order to get back, as far as possible, to the pure unarticulated and unexplained ground of direct experience. The direct experience of what? Life itself.'[13] Both Christians and Buddhists could practise Zen, 'if by Zen we mean precisely the quest for direct and pure experience on a metaphysical level, liberated from verbal formulas and linguistic preconceptions.'[14] Merton did not want to say that differences between religions are unimportant but that there is a common ground of reality from which they arise. He certainly never lost his own commitment to Christian theological understandings of God, and especially held firm to the central importance of the mystery of Christ and the collective life of Christ's body, the Church.

How to 'do' Zen, or what exactly Zen is, is hard to define. It is not a spiritual practice, or a form of belief. It is rather a wake-up call to open our eyes and see reality as it truly is. It is not a path to understanding but an invitation to sight – in more technical language Zen is an exploration of 'the natural ontological ground of being.'[15] Its most characteristic expression is through koans – stories or statements which are teasing and paradoxical forcing the hearer to go beyond rational understanding, and mondos – playful questions and answers between Zen masters and students which push the student to see things afresh. Zen pushes us to move outside our rational, logical minds to a place where our sight is not restricted by our preconceptions and our hearing is not deafened by our clamouring brains. In doing this it offers another pathway into the silence that Merton valued so greatly.

Zen helped Merton come to a place in his life where all the pretensions could be put aside and he could simply say of himself: 'What I wear is pants. What I do is live. How I pray is breathe.'[16] In the silence of the monastery, and finally of his hermitage, he was able to grow in generous compassion, living into the true calling of a monk: 'In reality the monk abandons the world only in order to listen more intently to the deepest and most neglected voices that proceed from its inner depths.'[17] Without silence Merton believed it would be impossible for anyone to live into their true self, or to discover the truth about the depth of God's love for all humanity. In this silence, as Merton said in one his last speeches made at the interfaith conference in Calcutta in October 1968, we find a unity which underlies all that divides praying people from one another:

The deepest level of communication is not communication, but communion. It is wordless. It is beyond words, and it is beyond speech, and it is beyond concept. Not that we discover a new unity. We discover an older unity. My dear brothers, we are already one. But we imagine that we are not. What we have to recover is our original unity. What we have to be is what we are.[18]

For Merton it is in silence that we discover our true nature, our true communion with one another, and our true union with that which is beyond all words: God, the ground of all being.

Exercise 2.3: Zen and silence

This is the story that Merton chose to begin and end his book *The Way of Chuang Tzu.*

Find a place of silence and solitude. Read through this story, not struggling to make sense of it but enjoying its rhythms and its humour. Embrace for yourself a patch of time in which you do nothing, not even try to pray, but just listen to the sounds around you, look at what is in front of your eyes and breathe in the air which gives you life.

One spring, as peach blossoms filled the valley below with a spray of white fragrance, an ancient sage wandered the Heights of Shang. There on a hillside stripped of everything else, he saw a large and extraordinary tree. So huge it was, the horses that drew a hundred chariots could be sheltered under its shade. 'What a tree this is!' he thought. Imagining the amount of timber it must contain, he marvelled that the tree had never been cut down.

But as he sat beneath it and looked up into the tree's branches, he saw how twisted and crooked they were. Turning in every direction, none of them were large enough to be made into rafters or beams. He reached up and broke off a twig, tasting the sap. It was sharp and bitter. 'This tree would be useless for tapping,' he concluded, 'producing no syrup of any worth.' The leaves, too, gave off an offensive odour as he broke them. They were too fragile to be woven into mats or braided into baskets. They would not even make good mulch! Even the roots, as he studied them, were so gnarled and knotty that one could never carve a bowl or fashion a fine decorative box out of them.

The sage said at last; 'This, indeed, is a tree good for nothing! That is why it has reached so great an age. The cinnamon tree can be eaten; so it is cut down. The varnish tree is useful, and therefore incisions are made in it. We all know the advantage of being useful, but only this tree knows the advantage of being useless!' The wise man sat in the shade of that great tree for the rest of the day, as a light wind drifted up from the valley below. He breathed the scent of distant peach blossoms and sat in studied silence, happily contemplating his own uselessness.

Questions for further reflection

(1) Within *The Cloud of Unknowing* and the writing of contemporary advocates of centering prayer there is an assumption that this is the highest form of prayer that a human being can achieve. Do you agree with this? What in this form of prayer sets it apart from other ways of praying?

(2) One of the defining factors of Christian spirituality is that it leads into loving action in the world, and is a communal spirituality shared with other members of the Body of Christ. Is there a danger that spiritualities of silence lead us away from loving service to others? If you disagree, how do you feel that these spiritualities enable the love of neighbour?

(3) Meister Eckhart, while resisting the teaching of a 'way' of prayer, emphasized the importance of an apophatic spirituality which gets behind all the names and images that we have of God. Do you believe it is possible to achieve a state where we put away all our names and images for the divine? A possible criticism of this

spirituality is that it leaves us with an abstract deity with whom it is impossible to see oneself in relationship, and also minimizes the revelatory work of Jesus Christ. How would you answer such critics if you disagree with them?

(4) Thomas Merton felt that his commitment to Christian faith was entirely compatible with the integration of a Zen approach into his spirituality. Do you feel that he was correct in this, or are you uncomfortable with his embrace of a way of thinking which originated within Buddhism? What do you feel are the possible dangers and/or advantages of Merton's integration of Zen?

Notes

1. *The Cloud of Unknowing*, ed. James Walsh, Society of Jesus, New York: Paulist Press, 1981, Chapter III, p.120.
2. *The Cloud of Unknowing*, Chapter II, p.119.
3. *Meditations with Meister Eckhart*, tr. and ed. Matthew Fox, Bear and Company: Santa Fe, 1983, p.44.
4. *Meditations with Meister Eckhart*, p.59.
5. Sermon 5b, in *Meister Eckhart: The Essential Sermons, Commentaries, Treatises and Defense*, tr. and intro. Edmund Colledge and Bernard McGinn, in the *Classics of Western Spirituality* series, Paulist Press: New York, 1981, p.183.
6. London: Sheldon Press, 1975 (1948).
7. Jim Forest, *Living with Wisdom: A Life of Thomas Merton*, Revised Edition, New York: Orbis Books, 2008 (1991), p.98.
8. From *Conjectures of a Guilty Bystander*, New York: Doubleday, 1966, p.140.
9. From a letter written in 1965, quoted in *Living with Wisdom*, p.187.
10. *The Sign of Jonas*, 24 May 1949, quoted in Henri Nouwen, *Pray to Live. Thomas Merton: Contemplative Critic*, Indiana: Fides Publications, 1972, pp.113–14.
11. *Thoughts in Solitude*, New York: Farrar, Straus and Giroux, 1956, p.69.
12. *Seeds of Contemplation* (re-named from *New Seeds of Contemplation* as Merton wished), Hertfordshire: Anthony Clarke Books, 1972 (1961), p.64. The use of male only language is typical of the era in which Merton wrote but does not reflect his view of the world in which the feminine aspect of God, and of humanity, had increasing importance.
13. *Zen and the Birds of Appetite*, New York: New Directions, 1968, p.36.
14. *Zen and the Birds of Appetite*, p.44.
15. *Zen and the Birds of Appetite*, p.45.
16. *A Thomas Merton Reader*, ed. Thomas P. McDonnell, New York: Doubleday, 1974, p.433.
17. Thomas Merton, *Contemplative Prayer*, New York: Image Books, 1971, p.23.
18. Quoted in *Living with Wisdom*, p.225.

Chapter 3

Creation and Creativity

When he established the heavens, I was there,
when he drew a circle on the face of the deep,
when he made firm the skies above,
when he established the fountains of the deep,
when he assigned to the sea its limit,
so that the waters might not transgress his command,
when he marked out the foundations of the earth,
then I was beside him, like a master worker;
and I was daily his delight,
rejoicing before him always,
rejoicing in his inhabited world
and delighting in the human race.

Wisdom speaking in Proverbs 8:27–31

The world has played many different roles within the history of Christian spirituality. It has been bracketed with 'the flesh and the devil' as the source of temptation and evil and, in this guise, is meant to be shunned by all trying to walk a Christian path. But it has also been believed to reveal the mysteries of God in a way that is second only to the more direct revelation of the Bible itself. Creation is believed to be both a distraction from the pursuit of God and a God-given aid for finding God. Throughout all this we can hear two different refrains clamouring for attention. The first, from Genesis 1, is 'God saw everything that he had made, and indeed, it was very good' (Genesis 1:31); the second, from 1 John, is 'Do not love the world or the things in the world. The love of the Father is not in those who love the world' (1 John 2:15).

Within the camp of those who celebrate created nature stands Thomas Traherne, the seventeenth-century English mystic:

> The brightness and magnificence of this world, which by reason of its height and greatness is hidden from men, is divine and wonderful. It addeth much to the glory of that temple in which we live. Yet it is the cause why men understand it not. They think it too great and wide to be enjoyed. But since it is all filled with the majesty of His glory who dwelleth in it; and the goodness of the Lord filleth the world, and His wisdom shineth everywhere within it and about it; and it aboundeth in an infinite variety of services, we need nothing but open eyes to be ravished like the cherubims. Well may we bear the greatness of the world, since it is our storehouse and treasury. That our treasures should be endless is an happy inconvenience: that all regions should be full of joys; and the room infinite wherein they are seated.[1]

While in the other camp stands Abba Arsenius, one of the Desert Fathers:

> One day Abba Arsenius came to a place where there were reeds blowing in the wind. The old man said to the brothers, 'What is this movement?' They said, 'Some reeds.' Then the old man said to them, 'When one who is living in silent prayer hears the song of a little sparrow, his heart no longer experiences the same peace. How much worse it is when you hear the movement of those reeds.[2]

In this chapter we stand with those who find value for our spiritual journey within the world of nature and look, in particular, at the Celtic and Franciscan traditions as well as contemporary eco-spirituality.

Remembering that we are co-creators with God the chapter will also look at the way that human creativity feeds into spirituality.

Celtic spirituality

God in Celtic Christianity is pictured not so much as the Lord of History as the Lord of Creation – the one whose wondrous works which we see all around us inspire praise and worship. Celtic prayers echo the psalms in their delight in the works of the Lord: 'Let us adore the Lord, Maker of wondrous works, Great bright heaven with its angels, The white waved sea on the earth' (Irish, ninth century). This aspect of their spirituality reflects the influence of the druidic traditions of the native peoples of the British Isles. Rivers, forests and hills throughout the country were believed to be dwelling places of divinity, and Christian missionaries often re-used such sacred sites for Christian places of worship: baptizing the local spirituality rather than attempting to simply eradicate it.

Stories abound of the special relationship that existed between Celtic saints and animals. St Cuthbert of Lindisfarne is famously supposed to have been dried off by otters after standing all night in the sea chanting psalms. He is also credited with conversations with the birds who were stealing his crops – allowing them the grain if they were in need of it, but telling them off for stealing it from him if they were not. St Brigit tamed and protected a wild boar, St Melangell saved a hare from the king's hunt, and St Columba commanded one of his monks to care for a crane who had been blown off-course onto Iona from Ireland. Celtic spirituality showed a care and concern for the non-human inhabitants of God's world, offering them the same hospitality and friendship that a human pilgrim could claim from them.

This attitude illustrates a sense that this life was good and full of potential, rather than that this life was fundamentally flawed and something which should be fled from. This beautiful poem, probably originating in ninth-century Ireland, talks of a humble near-paradise to be found in the here and now:

I wish, O Son of the living God,

O ancient, eternal King,

For a hidden little hut in the wilderness,

That it may be my dwelling.

An all-grey lithe little lark

To be by its side,

A clear pool to wash away sins

Through the grace of the Holy Spirit.

Quite near a beautiful wood

Around it on every side,

To nurse many-voiced birds,

Hiding it with its shelter.

A southern aspect for warmth,

A little brook across its floor,

A choice land with many precious gifts

Such as be good for every plant.[3]

It is no wonder that Celtic spirituality has gained a reputation as being more this-worldly, and more eco-friendly, than that of the Roman Church.

Celtic Christianity appears to view the created order as intrinsically good – and this included both the natural world and also human beings. The most characteristic theologian of the Celtic Church was Pelagius (c.350 to c.418 CE), a native of the British Isles. He is mainly known to us today through his controversy with Augustine of Hippo, who became seen as the champion of orthodoxy in opposition to

Pelagius' heresy. The main element of Pelagius' thought which relates to Celtic spirituality was his denial of the doctrine of original sin. Contrary to Augustine, Pelagius believed that sin is not an in-born characteristic of humanity but merely the result of our following Adam's bad example; indeed Pelagius stated: 'Evil is not born with us and we are procreated without fault' and taught that it was possible to see the face of God in that of a newborn child.

However, despite this positive approach to this world, we have to be careful before we ascribe our contemporary feelings about nature to people who lived many hundreds of years ago in a very different society from our own. There obviously was an appreciation of natural beauty, and a sense that animals and birds as well as humans were loved by God and should be treated with respect. But nature was not simply a benevolent friend. The natural world was also the place of encounter with monsters and demons. St Columba had the first documented run-in with the Loch Ness monster and the wilderness was known as the place where you went to in order to do battle with demons internal and external. This is why Celtic monasteries were built in wild and inaccessible places – not because of the wild beauty which makes them so appealing to modern sensibilities but because it was in such places that they could best do battle for God. Nature, for the Celts, was not a romantic notion but a daily reality: the source of food and delightful beauty but also the source of danger and potential death.

Exercise 3.1: Celtic Night Prayer

Let the light fade and the work be done
Let the flowers and the desk tops close
Let the sun go down and the world become still
And let the Son of God draw near

Blest be all creation
    And all that has life

Blest be the earth
    May it support our bed tonight
Blest be the fire
    May it glow in us tonight
Blest be the air
    May it make our night breath sweet

(There may be singing)

Psalm 104:1–4, 19–24 or other verses from this psalm

We give you thanks that you are always present, in all things,
each day and each night.
We give you thanks for your gifts of creation, life and friendship.
We give you thanks for the blessings of this day ...

(Any blessings may be named in silence or aloud)

When we are still we can sense you our Maker
We can feel your hand upon us
All that has been made stirs within us creation's song of praise.
Now we give you thanks for work completed
    We give you thanks for rest of night

(There may be silence or singing)
Genesis 1:3–5, 31a or words of Jesus

Guardian of the planets
Kindler of the stars
We pass into the darkness
Encompassed by you.
We offer you our concerns and the needs of your creation

(There may be prepared, silent or free prayer)

Thank you for your love for us, strong and nurturing
    We give back our lives to you
Thank you for our minds and bodies

We give back our lives to you
Thank you for the past day
    We give back our lives to you
After creation God rested
    We give back our lives to you
Protect us through the hours of this night,
be they silent or stormy,
that we who are wearied by the changes and chances of a restless
world
may rest upon you eternally.
You created the world out of love
    Now we return to you in love.
Let us rest in God this night.
    And awake in newness of life.[4]

The rhythms of life

An awareness of the rhythms of the day and the year is very much
a part of Celtic spirituality, and one that reveals something of both
its rural and its monastic roots. Celtic Christianity was spread and
nurtured by local monastic communities rather than by local parish
churches. The great saints of the Celtic Church were all monastics:
Columba, Hilda, Aidan, Patrick, David, Brigid and Cuthbert were all
heads of monasteries as well as teachers, soul friends and missionaries. The Christianity that they brought to the people was one that
was rooted in the pattern of monastic daily prayer, with offices
marking the beginning of the day, noon and evening and the
preparation for sleep. Each part of the day was hallowed by being
consciously considered as lived in the presence, and under the
protection, of God.

This sense of the hallowedness of the different parts of the day
can be found in the prayers of the Carmina Gadelica. These prayers,
songs and poems were collected by Alexander Carmichael at the
end of the nineteenth century from the oral tradition of the western

Scottish islands and highlands. There is, obviously, a considerable length of time separating them from the period of the Celtic church and their provenance is limited to only one geographical area of the Celtic world; all of which serves as a note of caution before they are taken as precise evidence of the beliefs of Celtic Christians from the fifth to ninth centuries CE. However, they do seem to contain a residual flavour of the Celtic way of looking at the world, and at time as part of that world.

The whole day began with the hallowing of prayer, most often through the invocation of the presence and protection of the Trinity, as in this simple prayer:

> *I am bending my knee*
> *In the eye of the Father who created me,*
> *In the eye of the Son who purchased me,*
> *In the eye of the Spirit who cleansed me,*
> *In friendship and affection.*[5]

There were special prayers for the different tasks of the day; this first for getting dressed:

> *Even as I clothe my body with wool*
> *Cover Thou my soul with the shadow of Thy wing.*[6]

and the second for clipping sheep:

> *Go shorn and come woolly,*
> *Bear the Beltane female lamb,*
> *Be the lovely Bride thee endowing,*
> *And the fair Mary thee sustaining,*
> *The fair Mary sustaining thee.*
> *Michael the chief be shielding thee*
> *From the evil dog and from the fox,*
> *From the wolf and from the sly bear,*

And from the taloned birds of destructive bills,
From the taloned birds of hooked bills.[7]

The day also ended with prayer and the seeking of the protection of
God in sleep:

I am lying down to-night
With Mary mild and with her Son,
With the Mother of my King,
Who is shielding me from harm.
  I will not lie down with evil,
  Nor shall evil lie down with me,
  But I will lie down with God,
  And God will lie down with me.
God and Mary and Michael kindly
And the cross of the nine angels fair,
Be shielding me as Three and as One,
From the brow of my face to the edge of my soles.[8]

The whole rhythm of the day was patterned with prayer, the under-
lying assumption being that God would be concerned in the minutiae
of one's life: a life where there was no hard and fast division between
the sacred and the secular.

There is also within the Celtic tradition of spirituality a recognition of the ebb and flow of life both across the year and across the
years. The former is part of the spiritual life of the whole Church as
the liturgical year marks the turning of the seasons, with festivals
such as Harvest and Thanksgiving linking the Church's year to that
of the working world. The importance of the Church's seasons in the
early years of Christianity in Britain can be seen in the discomfort
caused by the different dating systems for Easter between the Celtic
and Roman traditions. It was felt to be a scandal that within the
same household some members would be still holding the Lenten
fast while others were already tucking into the Easter feast. It was

important that communities as well as families should move through the year together, united in their periods of penitence and rejoicing, at one with one another.

There has been more interest recently in the different spiritual seasons of life, with a wish to mark and remark upon the changes that seem to follow the human aging process. In particular a recognition that the middle years of life often bring with them a turn inwards, with fulfilment and satisfaction being seen to have less to do with acquisitions and achievements and more to do with a sense of purpose and meaning to life. The early years of adult life are seen as being concerned with success in its outward forms: finding security in work and in establishing one's place within society through relationships and status, with creativity focused outwards on accomplishments and on the birthing and raising of children. When all this has been achieved there is often a perception that something is still missing or, perhaps, an inner restlessness that refuses to completely go away. This change does not happen in everyone and, when it does, may not be predicted in purely chronological terms – some begin their inner journey in their thirties, some in their sixties, and some never begin at all.

Many cultures recognize that the later years of life are the time when wisdom is garnered and spiritual stories are retold with new resonance and power. It is this spiritual maturity which is seen to give worth to members of the family and nation whose productivity is passed. Older folk are not seen as being of little worth because their active life is slowing down, but of greater worth because their inner life is gaining complexity and depth. It is never too late, nor too early, to start considering what is of ultimate importance and ultimate meaning in one's life, and to begin living out that recognition in the choices that one makes. For some, as will be seen in our next section, the questions and the answers come early, and with dramatic consequences.

Franciscan spirituality

Franciscan spirituality cannot be understood apart from the figure of St Francis. It is not a spirituality that is noted for a particular way of prayer but rather one that is noted for a particular attitude to the world – an attitude inherited directly from the personality and charism of its founder. There are three central components of this spiritual attitude: a love for volitional poverty, an incarnational understanding of the natural world and a commitment to work for justice, peace and reconciliation. These three can all be seen quite clearly within Francis' life and the choices that he made.

Francis was born to a wealthy family in the city of Assisi in 1181 or 1182 and he died near there on 3 October 1226. His father, Pietro Bernardone, was a wealthy cloth merchant; of his mother, Pica, little is known, but she is said to have belonged to a noble family of Provence. There was family wealth to spare for their son's amusements: which included fighting against rival Italian cities, a pastime which led to Francis spending some time as a prisoner of war. He was generally known as one of the lads, enjoying the trappings that came with wealth and showing no desire to settle down to work – or to prayer.

A series of events changed Francis' direction in life radically. One of the first of these was an encounter with a leper. Francis was a fastidious young man who enjoyed good clothes and appreciated beauty. He also avoided the smell, disfigurement and squalor that accompanied the life of lepers – preferring not even to look at the leper hospital nearby. Then, so the legend goes, riding out of the city one day he encountered a leper in the road. Instead of averting his eyes and riding by, as he would normally have done, Francis felt a compulsion to get down from his horse and approach the man. He even kissed the leper's deformed hand. In this leper Francis believed that he had met Christ; and he began to understand that the worth of a human being was not defined by fine clothing and status but was inherent in the very fact of being created in the image of

God, however imperfect the body that held that image. Christ was revealed in the poverty of the leper rather than hidden by the man's deformity.

This was the start of Francis' love affair with 'Lady Poverty' who eventually enticed him away from his privileged but purposeless life. His most dramatic gesture of love towards her was to strip naked of all his clothes in the town square in Assisi, discarding the wealth and position that came to him from birth. At the same time he disowned Pietro, his father, so that he could be totally obedient to his Heavenly Father. Francis felt that radical, voluntary poverty was a necessary prerequisite for truly following in the footsteps of Christ; taking seriously the gospel command to proclaim the kingdom of God as given to the disciples: 'Take nothing for your journey, no staff, nor bag, nor bread, nor money – not even an extra tunic' (Luke 9:3). Francis chose a life stripped not only of luxury but of basic security in order to walk more closely in the footsteps of Christ, the one who gave up everything to walk with us.

Francis' relationship with the natural world arose out of his relationship with God, and especially with the person of Jesus. Francis' spirituality was profoundly incarnational: focused on the way that God was revealed in the life of Jesus of Nazareth and continues to be revealed through Christ's continuing presence in the world. It is appropriate that Francis is credited with the introduction of the Christmas crib celebrating the human birth of Jesus; and was also said to have the stigmata – the five wounds of the crucifixion – manifested on his own body. The Jesus of the gospels was not a distant figure for Francis but a constant inspiration, and also someone whose presence was to be encountered in other human beings and in the natural world more widely. Francis' vision of God was of a creator still intimately concerned with his creation and whose compassion was directed to all created beings and not exclusively to humanity.

There is room here for only one of the many stories of Francis' encounters with animals that expresses this relationship: that with the wolf of Gubbio. The story goes that the town of Gubbio was being terrorized by a fierce wolf who attacked men and women along with domestic animals. Francis, against the advice of the townspeople, went out to meet the wolf; who charged at him with his fierce mouth open to attack. However, when Francis made the sign of the cross the wolf became as gentle as a lamb, submitting to Francis and offering his paw to shake as a sign that he would no longer attack the townsfolk. Francis' concern, however, was not limited to the human beings – he also ensured that 'Brother Wolf' would be cared for by his former victims. The story has a happy ending for both wolf and people: 'From that day, the wolf and the people kept the pact which St. Francis made. The wolf lived two years more, and it went from door to door for food. It hurt no one, and no one hurt it The people fed it courteously. And it is a striking fact that not a single dog ever barked at it.' Francis was not satisfied till the needs of all God's creatures – human and vulpine – had been met.

Franciscan spirituality continues to have a commitment to the discovery of God's love in nature and an openness to the possibility of all creation being called to honour and to worship God. Contemporary Franciscans may not preach to the birds, but they would see it as part of their spiritual work to protect and nurture the birds of the air, along with the fish of the sea and all the creatures of the land. All creatures are created by God and, as God's handiwork, deserve to be treated respectfully. Even more than this, all animals are capable of giving praise to God according to their nature – so birds singing, roses blooming and greyhounds running are all a source of delight to God as well as to human beings. The earth is indeed full of the glory of God and it is humanity's duty to shepherd the earth in such a way that this glory increases rather than diminishes.

There are three particular ways in which Franciscan spirituality responds to this imperative to care for God's world. The first is the most obvious – like its founder, Franciscans continue to take delight in the world around them and see it as a place of beauty and revelation. *The Canticle of the Sun*, one of Francis' best-known and best-loved prayers, continues to inform the Franciscan attitude to the natural world:

> *Be praised, my Lord, through all your creatures, especially through my lord Brother Sun, who brings the day; and you give light through him. And he is beautiful and radiant in all his splendour! Of you, Most High, he bears the likeness.*
>
> *Be praised, my Lord, through Sister Moon and the stars; in the heavens you have made them, precious and beautiful.*
>
> *Be praised, my Lord, through Brothers Wind and Air, and clouds and storms, and all the weather, through which you give your creatures sustenance.*
>
> *Be praised, My Lord, through Sister Water; she is very useful, and humble, and precious, and pure.*[9]

Franciscan spirituality is open to the delight of nature and aware of the presence of God within the world: the immanent God as much as the transcendent God.

The second way that Franciscan spirituality honours the natural world is through a commitment to simplicity – the more liveable-with interpretation of Francis' single-minded, and single-hearted, devotion to Lady Poverty. This involves a commitment to limit your consumption to what you need rather than to what you covet: a philosophy of thankfulness for what you have rather than of aspiration for what a few other people have. Another way of looking at this is as a commitment to taking up no more room on the earth than is appropriate for you: being aware of the millions of others who make this earth their home and working hard not to squeeze their needs out of the way. This is a spirituality that can easily lead one into working for a fairer distribution of the world's resources, as well as working for a world which is far more ecologically aware and ecologically responsible. Like all authentic Christian spirituality, the Franciscan path is as much about how your way of life makes life better for others as it is about finding a way that is personally fulfilling for you as an individual.

The third way that Franciscan spirituality continues to live out God's care for the world is through a commitment to peace and justice. Francis himself tried, without great success, to bring to an end the siege of Damietta in Egypt in 1219 during the Fifth Crusade. Because they see God's image and beauty reflected in all the things that God has made, those who follow Franciscan spirituality have a particular commitment to seeing all people flourish; and a practical awareness that such flourishing is most likely under conditions of peace and freedom from oppression. Franciscan spirituality looks to break down barriers between people, and peoples, so that it is possible for each to see the God-given beauty in the other and move forwards with mutual respect even where there is continued disagreement. Franciscan work to make peace can perhaps be seen as the story of the Wolf of Gubbio lived out in many different arenas.

The key to Franciscan spirituality is that it does not call you to a particular set of spiritual practices or see itself as the highest path to God. Instead it calls people to consider carefully the choices they make in life and to see these choices as directly tied in to their relationship with God. Franciscan spirituality, in other words, is more about what you do than how you pray. It invites an attitude of joy and thanksgiving in response to the natural world; and a consequent passion to see all of God's creation, including men and women, protected, nurtured and enabled to flourish. There is an acceptance that, for this to happen, individuals may have to make choices which go against the dominant consumer culture of the developed world and limit one's consumption of the world's finite resources. Heroic voluntary poverty may not be a calling for many, but simplicity of life is a recurrent value within Christian spiritual thinking and a more realistic goal for most of us.

Exercise 3.2: A prayer walk

A prayer walk is all about spending some time with God in the natural world, nothing to do with getting from A to B. It can be as short or as long as you are comfortable with – and if you find walking difficult it could, instead, be a time spent sitting outdoors. Choose a place where you can meander comfortably – your garden, a city park, a country path or wherever you feel at ease.

As you walk or sit, allow all your senses to be at work.

Take time to look at what is around you, pausing to examine in detail any leaf or flower or stone that catches your attention.

Take time to listen to any sounds that are around – birdsong, or children's chatter, wind or running water.

Take time to become aware of the sensation of touch. Feel the sun, wind or rain on your face, handle gently flowers and leaves, feel the roughness or smoothness of a tree's bark.

Take time to enjoy – or notice – the scents of nature. These might be purely pleasurable, like the scent from a rose, or more earthy like the smell of sheep, cows and manure.

Take time, if you can, to taste something of nature. Bring a piece of fruit or some nuts with you to eat.

As you become aware of the intricacies and beauties of life around you allow your awareness to turn to prayer. You might thank the creator for creation, you might want to lament humanity's misuse of the world, you might want to sing and dance in joy and praise. Pray in whatever way feels appropriate and natural for you.

You might want to bring a reminder of the walk home with you – a fallen leaf, a shell or a pebble (only pick a flower if it belongs to you). This could be a focus for continued prayer on another occasion.

Contemporary eco-spirituality

There has been a growing awareness within Western society in recent years of the disastrous impact that human development is having on the planet entrusted to our care. This knowledge has impacted on the field of Christian spirituality and led to a new commitment to an ecologically aware and responsible way of living as a necessary part of Christian faith. Along with a practical commitment to simplicity of life, which closely follows in the steps of Franciscan spirituality, there has been a new assessment of humanity's relationship with the rest of the created world – something often particularly apparent in the works of feminist eco-theologians and writers of spirituality.

The traditional Christian view of creation is to see it as of value and worth both because it has been created by God and because it is serviceable for us in enabling our material, and therefore also our spiritual, lives. Creation is of use and for use, to be tended as a resource from a position of responsible stewardship. This is probably where many Christians still are today in their attitude to the natural world. However there are many Christians who would put the relationship very differently. Rather than seeing the natural world as a pyramid, with non-living matter at the base and humanity at the pinnacle, many Christians now talk of a 'web of life' in which all created matter plays a particular, and irreplaceable, part. It is an image of inter-dependence, acknowledging more fully humanity's own material, animal nature.

Within this schema, the natural world is not seen primarily as a resource for humanity but as of worth in its own right: valuable simply for what it is rather than for what it is for. It is no longer believed to be acceptable that species should fall victim to our need for the resources that enable the high-consumption culture of the wealthy and developed areas of the world. The planet is worth preserving for itself rather than only for ourselves and our children.

This changed perspective to the natural world can be seen in the current enthusiasm for an emphasis on the immanence rather than the transcendence of God. In other words, an emphasis on the idea that God is present within us and within creation rather than on the idea that God is beyond all created things. This, it should be noted, is a change of emphasis rather than a denial that both immanence and transcendence are aspects of the God experienced within Christian spirituality. Sallie McFague, for example, talks of the world as 'God's body' in a panentheistic theological worldview. This sees God as present within, but also transcendent of, the created world as opposed to pantheism which sees God as entirely held within the material universe. It is worth quoting her 'Call to Action' in full as it is both a deeply ethical and a deeply spiritual challenge:

> The Ecological Reformation is the great work before us. The urgency of this task is difficult to overstate. We do not have centuries to turn ourselves around and begin to treat our planet and our poorer brothers and sisters differently. We may not even have the next century. But the scales are falling from our eyes and we see what we must do. We must change how we think about ourselves and we must act on that new knowledge. We must see ourselves as radically dependent on nature and as supremely responsible for it. And most of all, we North American privileged people who are consuming many times our share at the table must find ways to restructure our society, our nation, and the world toward great equitability. Christians should be at the forefront of this great work – and it is a *great* work. Never before have people had to think about the well-being of the entire planet – we did not ask for this task, but it is the one being demanded of us. We Christians must participate in the agenda the planet has set before us – in public and prophetic ways – as our God 'who so loved the world' would have us do.[10]

Part of the way that we can make this Ecological Reformation more likely is through cultivating a spirituality which values the material as well as the spiritual. The material world is not the enemy of the spiritual life but its necessary foundation and milieu: we do not become spiritually mature in order to flee the world but in order to serve God in and through the world. This world is the place we encounter God and it is this whole universe, not just humanity alone, that is God's beloved creation. A spirituality which fails to act responsibly in the light of this insight is one that has failed to be fully true to its Christian calling.

Creativity and prayer

One of the ways that human beings have expressed their spirituality throughout history and throughout different cultures, is through their own artistic creativity. This can be in the form of spirit masks, of tribal dances, of icons, of poetry, of sacred architecture, of music – the list is bounded only by the limits of human imagination. The spiritual urge to explore the deepest truths and potential of what it means to be fully human finds a natural companion in the creative urge to express these deepest truths and potentialities. Producing works of art that are able to communicate something of this deep reality may be beyond the reach of most of us, however the least artistically gifted of us can still find ways in which human creativity enriches and enlivens our own spiritual journey.

I, for instance, grew up being told that art was not my thing. My drawings of people never progressed beyond the stick-figure stage and I still cringe with embarrassment if I am coerced into playing *Pictionary*. I well remember the art class when my (eccentric and delightful) art teacher told me that, rather than drawing the daffodil like the rest of the class, it would be enough for me to contemplate it. For most of my life, therefore, it did not occur to me to use any visual creativity as part of prayer: drawing and art was associated with failure, even though I continued to gain much from my appreciation of other people's art. My epiphany in this matter came when a spiritual director invited me to try drawing using my non-dominant hand – in my case my left hand. I knew that I was not expected to be able to produce anything 'worthy' with this hand and so felt free to play with colour and shape; concentrating on the process of putting prayer into a visual medium rather than obsessed with what the final product looked like. And, to be honest, the final product was no more worthy of objective praise than anything else I had ever painted. The difference was that this no longer mattered: the art had been part of a process of prayer not an attempt to produce something that others would praise.

Using painting – or drawing or clay – is one way in prayer of getting out of your head and into your emotions and your gut. Rather than striving to find the right word to express your feeling to God you can find the right colour or line or shape to do this and, in the process, the hands and body become part of the prayer practice. Painting in prayer never needs to strive to be worthy of God – like all our prayer it needs merely to be honest and open to God's presence. Occasionally I find I end up with something that continues to speak to me after the prayer session is over but often it is enough just to have found another way of being with God in that prayer time. I know musicians who speak of their practice time as when they are most at prayer, finding in the focus on the process the space to focus on God.

Art produced by other people is also a way into prayer for many people, whether this was the original intention of the artist or not. Although this is certainly the case for the visual arts, and for poetry, it is perhaps most noticeable with music. Research shows that, after listening to music of any sort, the human heart generally beats at a slower pace. Music heightens our mood as well as providing a protective barrier between us and more intrusive, distracting sounds. Part of the attraction of hymn singing is their ability to open our emotions to God, this is also the gift of music that we listen to on our own or produce through our own playing. Indeed, for some people music is the necessary backdrop to prayer, a prerequisite for quieting the mind and moving to a place of inner stillness. There should be no internal 'taste police' dictating the sort of music we ought to find fulfils this role for us: for some people it will be classical, for others specifically Christian and for others contemporary music from Trance to country ballads. We use whatever music leads us into contemplation, prayer or praise rather than whatever music would impress our peers and receive critical acclaim. As Jesus taught, prayer is not an opportunity to show-off but a time to step aside from busyness and be with God (Matthew 6:5–6).

It would be improper to talk about creativity and prayer without some mention, however compressed, of the role of icons. These are more than works of art that lead us into prayer, they are works of prayer themselves that lead both the one who writes them (icons are 'written' rather than 'painted') and the one who regards them into an awareness of the presence of God. They have been an integral part of the spirituality of the Orthodox churches for well over a thousand years and have found a new place within Western spirituality over the last decades. Far more than portraits of holy people – whether Jesus Christ, the Blessed Virgin Mary or a particular saint – they are glimpses of the face of God seen through the lens of a human face. The colours and attitudes used are highly symbolic: both gold and red, for example, are representative of divinity while blue and green stand for the earth and humanity. The fact that there are no shadows within icons speaks of Christ's light flooding the universe, leaving no darkness unilluminated. Prayer with icons is an invitation into visual contemplation that brings with it a consciousness of the presence of God and may evoke awareness of a particular aspect of God's nature: nurturing love as seen in icons of the Blessed Virgin Mary and the Christ Child, triumph over evil as seen in icons of St George or wisdom as seen in icons of Hagia Sophia (Holy Wisdom). In all cases, icons are windows into the nature of God, not pieces of decorative art to adorn museums or living rooms.

Exercise 3.3: Prayer with the creative spirit

(i)   Choose some music which you find leads you into a prayerful or reflective frame of mind.

(ii) Prepare some simple art materials – a piece of plain paper and some coloured pencils, pens or pastels are all you need.

(iii)   Sit and listen quietly, opening yourself to the music and focusing on that alone.

(iv)   When you feel ready, take a pencil with your non-dominant hand (the left if you are right-handed, the right if you are left-handed) and begin to draw whatever the music is making you feel. Don't be concerned with producing anything worthy to be shown to others; in fact, don't focus on the end product at all but only on the process. Remember – no one can be expected to produce a masterpiece with their non-dominant hand. Change the colour you are using as often as feels right.

(v)   When you feel you have finished, spend some time looking at the pattern or picture you have produced and see whether it speaks to you of God, or the music, or where you are spiritually at the moment.

(vi)   Close by thanking God for the gifts of creativity in all its forms.

Questions for further reflection

(1)   Both Celtic spirituality and eco-spirituality emphasize the importance of this world as a place of encounter with God. Do you see any dangers in this emphasis? For instance, some Christians feel that, because the world has fallen away from its original goodness, it can no longer be truly revelatory of God. Would you agree?

(2)   St Francis was in love with Lady Poverty and viewed being without possessions as essential to living a life that truly followed in Jesus' footsteps. Do you agree that material wealth gets in the way of living a Christian life? Do you ever feel torn between the desire for financial security for yourself and your family and your wish to live a life of more radical commitment to the gospel? How do you, or how might you, reconcile this tension – or is it beyond reconciliation?

(3)   Do you believe that the creativity of humanity can mirror the creativity of the divine Creator, or does our involvement in

a sinful world mean that we are too damaged to make this possible?

Notes

1. Thomas Traherne, *Centuries of Meditation*: The First Century, 37 in *Selected Poems and Prose*, London: Penguin, 1991, pp.200–1.
2. Ward, Benedicta, *The Sayings of the Desert Fathers*, Kalamazoo: Cistercian Publications, 1975, p.13.
3. Quoted in Esther de Waal, *The Celtic Way of Prayer*, Second Edition, London: Hodder and Stoughton, 2003 (1996), pp.86–7.
4. This order of Celtic Night Prayer is taken from the Community of Aidan and Hilda.
5. Quoted in Esther de Waal, *The Celtic Way of Prayer*, p.67.
6. Quoted in Esther de Waal, *The Celtic Way of Prayer*, p.69.
7. Carmina Gadelica, I, Labour, 100, Beannachd Lombaidh.
8. Carmina Gadelica, I, Invocations, 37, Beannachadh Leapa.
9. These are four of the nine stanzas of the prayer.
10. Sallie McFague, *Life Abundant: Rethinking Theology and Economy for a Planet in Peril*, Minneapolis: Fortress Press, 2001, p.210.

Chapter 4

Wilderness

Jesus, full of the Holy Spirit, returned from the Jordan
and was led by the Spirit in the wilderness.

Luke 4:1

It is only since moving to the west coast of Canada that I have personally come into contact with wilderness in its classic sense of uncultivated and uninhabited land. England has been the home of too many people for too many generations for there to be any sizeable areas left where you can be unaware of the presence of other human beings and the works of human civilization. Even when out of the sight and sound of cars there are likely to be dry-stone-walls or paint-marked sheep to remind you that the countryside has been tamed and adapted to fit human needs. However in British Columbia it is possible, even within a short distance of the city, to look out on miles of forest unmarked by buildings, roads or agriculture where bears and cougars still threaten human life and where you can easily imagine yourself lost and isolated. Nature does not look or feel tamed and safe. You are reminded of the vulnerability of your human body and that we are not, despite our recurrent hubris, masters of all we survey.

Wilderness both threatens and beckons within the Christian tradition. It is a place where you confront the realities of life, both positive and negative: a place of black and white rather than of shades of grey. It is harder for both virtue and evil to hide their true nature within the emptiness of the wilderness: there is a sense of life being stripped to its essentials without the usual clutter of daily living covering up the truth of things. Choices are more extreme in the wilderness, and so are the potential rewards and the potential costs. Wilderness is a place both of epiphany – encounter with God – and of temptation, as evil is confronted both without and within.

Within the biblical narrative wilderness occurs again and again as a place of encounter and of testing. Hagar, driven into the desert by the harsh treatment she received from her mistress Sarah, is met and comforted by God who she names 'El-roi', the God who sees. Moses is confronted by God in the burning bush when he has led his flock away into the wilderness and finds that here is sacred ground. He then leads the Israelites out from slavery into a wilderness which offers both freedom and also hardship. It is only after they have survived this inhospitable landscape for forty years, during which they learn more of God and also more of their own propensity to stray from God, that they are called to enter into the 'promised land'. It is to the wilderness that the prophets retreat when they need to clear their vision and to listen for the voice of God away from the noise of village or city.

The wilderness features most famously in the New Testament as the place where Jesus encounters and overcomes temptation. Immediately after the Holy Spirit affirms his identity as God's beloved Son at his baptism, Jesus is led by the same Spirit 'into the wilderness to be tempted by the devil' (Matthew 4:1) or, as Mark's gospel puts it, 'And the Spirit immediately drove him out into the wilderness' (Mark 1:12). It is worth emphasizing that it is the Spirit and not the devil which leads Jesus into the wilderness – it is a place where he needs to spend time before he can properly begin his ministry. Indeed, it is while spending forty days here that Jesus comes to terms with his own identity and begins to understand what it means to be the Messiah. The biblical writers describe this in terms of Jesus' victory over the wiles of the devil: the wilderness becomes a site of spiritual warfare, a theme which echoes through the later wilderness tradition.

Whether it is a place of encounter with angels or with demons, the Bible suggests that the wilderness is not a place that can be avoided on the spiritual journeys of the people of God. It is not our final destination but it is a necessary stage on the pilgrimage. It can be comforting and encouraging to know this when we have our own wilderness experiences: this is a place where God's people have always walked and where they have found God. It may be that the Spirit is leading us into our wilderness in order that we too can find God, and ourselves, anew.

The Desert Fathers and Mothers

The Desert Fathers and Mothers is the collective name for a group of Christians who were a phenomenon in the Church in the third and fourth centuries. As their name suggests, they are remembered for their choice to move outside the boundaries of established communities and seek a new life in wilderness and desert places. Their range extended through the deserts of Egypt, Palestine and Syria and they are best known to us today through the contemporary collections of their sayings and of the stories of their lives. It is fair to say that they were mostly Fathers or, at least, that it is mostly Fathers that we know about today: in the collection of their lives there is no mention of female hermits, while the collected sayings include only three women among 127 men.

Their particular spirituality came about in response to the changing nature of the Church at that time. Before 300 BCE, becoming a Christian was a dangerous choice to make. The risk of persecution and martyrdom was real – although the degree of risk varied with the vagaries of different emperors – and it was possible to live a spiritually beleaguered life within the confines of normal civilization. The Church was the under-dog and being a Christian meant stepping outside the norms of society – it was a counter-cultural choice. The change came as Christianity first became respectable and then embraced as the official religion of the Empire; Emperor Constantine accepting Christianity, so the legend goes, after seeing a vision of the cross on a battle-field where he was then victorious. Finding privations as a Christian became harder and it was no longer realistic to expect the crown of martyrdom to be offered to you. Christianity was now identified with the official culture rather than in opposition to it.

This was problematic for a number of Christians who understood Christianity as a faith that should be world denying and prophetic rather than world affirming and conformist. They felt that there needed to be some grit within the Christian life to produce the pearl of proper service to God. They had also been taught that martyrdom was the surest way to heaven. So, seeking a new way of discipline and appropriate hardship, some Christians began a move out into the wilderness: a place which they knew from the Bible was likely to bring them into encounter with angels and demons and even with God's very self.

The most famous of these desert seekers was St Antony of Egypt, who is credited with being the founding father of monasticism. This, however, was not Antony's original intention: he went into the wilderness to be a hermit rather than to found a monastic community. At first Antony was content to dwell among the tombs outside the city walls – long believed to be the haunt of demons and, therefore, an appropriate site for a spiritual warrior. However as more people sought his teaching and his prayers, he eventually felt it necessary to move further out into the desert itself. His desire was to find a place where he could be alone with God, engaged in cleansing his own soul – battling his own demons – and interceding for the salvation of his fellow Christians. In practice he was thwarted by the reputation for holiness that his way of life won him, as less hardy Christians flocked to hear his teaching and some of the more hardy begged to become his desert disciples.

The fact that Antony and the other Fathers and Mothers never achieved the isolation that was their dream is attested to by the fact that we can still read some of their words today. They themselves realized also that the Christian life could never be one of complete withdrawal and separation from the world: it must still be lived in service to one's neighbours whether through active helping or intercession, recognizing in the face of the stranger the face of Christ:

> Abba Apollo said, 'When you have seen your brother, you have seen the Lord your God.

They also knew that the Christian life could be well lived within the confines of everyday life:

> It was revealed to Abba Anthony in the desert that there was one who was his equal in the city. He was a doctor by profession and whatever he had beyond his needs he gave to the poor, and every day he sang the Sanctus with the angels.

The Desert Fathers and Mothers recognized that their way of life wasn't for everyone and didn't deny that it was possible to follow God faithfully in other circumstances. They were, however, seen as the athletes and champions of the spiritual life, and valued as such by the citizens of the cities. Their presence was considered to provide a protective barrier of prayer almost as effective and necessary as the physical city walls.

The successors to the Desert Fathers and Mothers can be found in a number of different places. Most obviously, all the monastic orders that succeeded them are based on a model of withdrawal from the norms of society in order to serve God and that society in a particular way. More particularly, the focus on wilderness is apparent in the sites selected for Celtic monasteries in the British Isles. We see places such as Iona and Lindisfarne as unspoilt and picturesque but they were originally chosen less for their beauty than for the isolation and physical challenge that they offered. The wild places were still believed to be the haunt of demons and, therefore, a perfect arena for those engaged in spiritual warfare.

There are still those, of course, who seek wilderness today – as the number of retreat houses in North America and beyond offering 'wilderness spiritual experiences' shows. But the encounter often looked for is one with the self rather than one either with demons or with God. Wilderness is still seen as a place of black and white where civilized pretence is stripped away, but the reality to be found under that pretence is more likely to be interpreted in terms of self-awareness or getting in touch with the universal spirit than in terms of spiritual warfare and humility. The beauty of the wilderness now predominates over its wildness and danger and it is used more as a site for vacations from the stresses of real life than as a place to live out one's spiritual calling.

The sayings of the Desert Fathers and Mothers

The Desert Fathers and Mothers continue to influence Christian spirituality today mainly through their recorded sayings. These sayings are challenging, didactic, earthy, occasionally humorous, sometimes dated, sometimes timeless. They deal with questions about prayer, about spiritual formation, about the essentials of the Christian life, about how to treat the body and about how to achieve perfection. The two most common contexts for these sayings are a master instructing his or her disciples or a master recalling the perfections and teachings of another father or mother. The following gives only a taste of these sayings and of some of the main categories into which they fall. They are best read meditatively, allowing space between the sayings so that they may each have a chance to speak their teaching clearly – and to give the reader space to accept or reject the saying as a spiritual truth for them.

Stability

The Desert Fathers and Mothers looked for discipline and stability in their disciples, as well as in their own lives. They taught that one would learn more from staying in one place and letting God find one there rather than wandering far and wide searching for God. In our contemporary world, where it seems that people are always on the move, it is good to be reminded that we do not have to go looking for God but that God will find us wherever we may be:

> Blessed Syncletica said: 'If you find yourself in a monastery, do not go to another place. For that will harm you a great deal. Just as the bird that abandons the eggs she was sitting on prevents them from hatching, do the monk or the nun grow cold and their faith dies, when they go from one place to the other.'[1]

> Abba John the Dwarf gave this advice: 'Watching means to sit in your cell and always be mindful of God. This is what is meant by the words: 'I was on the watch, and God came to me' (cf Matt 25.36).'

> A brother came to Scetis to visit Abba Moses and asked him for a word. The old man said to him: 'Go, sit in your cell, and your cell will teach you everything.'

Silence

One of the great gifts of the desert to its monks and nuns was the possibility of silence. They wanted the peace and quiet to be able to listen to the voice of God, and to their own inner voice. Silence was a way of opening themselves up to the reality of God and, as they saw it, to a realization of their distance from God. Speech was a distraction and also a source of temptation – both for boasting or exaggeration and for idle chatter which took one's mind away from the profundities of repentance and faith.

> Abba Macarius said to the brothers at Scetis: 'Flee, my brothers.' One of the old men asked him: 'Where else could we flee beyond this desert?' Macarius placed his finger on his lips and said: 'Flee that.' And he went into his cell, shut the door, and sat down.

It was said of Abba Agathon that for three years he lived with a stone in his mouth, until he had learnt to keep silence.

Abba Poemen said: 'Someone may seem to be silent, but if in the heart one is condemning others, then one is babbling ceaselessly. And there may be another person who talks from morning till evening, and yet in the heart that person is truly silent. That person says nothing that is not profitable.'

Having withdrawn to the desert, Abba Arsenius ... heard a voice saying to him: 'Arsenius, flee; be silent; pray always. These are the source of sinlessness.'

Prayer

The point of both stability in the cell and silence was in order to facilitate a constant stream of prayer. This was the work of the desert monks and nuns – to pray for their own salvation and for the salvation of their fellow men and women. Prayer was intended to be as near constant as it was possible to make it and was understood as the best path to both humility and holiness.

Abba Isidore said: 'When I was younger and remained in my cell, I set no limit to prayer. The whole night was for me as much a time of prayer as the day.'

Abba Macarius was asked: 'How should one pray?' The old man replied: 'There is no need at all to make long discourses. It is enough to stretch out one's hands and to say: "Lord, as you will, and as you know, have mercy." And if the conflict grows fiercer, say: "Lord, help!" He knows very well what we need and He shows us His mercy.'

Abba Lot went to see Abba Joseph and said to him: 'Abba, as far as I can I say my little office, I fast a little, I pray and meditate, I live in peace and, again as far as I can, I purify my thoughts.

What else can I do?' Then, the old man stood up and stretched his hands toward heaven. His fingers became like ten lamps of fire, and he said to him: 'If you really want, you can become all flame.'

Love

Although the Desert Fathers and Mothers sought solitude, they did not forget that the command to love one's neighbour followed directly from the command to love God. They realized that with no encounter with other people there would be no-one's feet for them to wash, no way to imitate the service that characterized Christ's life. So, although they could be demanding and harsh, they could also be gentle and patient.

One day when Abba John was going up to Scetis with some other brothers, their guide lost his way for it was night-time. So the brothers said to Abba John, 'What shall we do, abba, in order not to die wandering about, for the brother has lost the way?' The old man said to them, 'If we speak to him he will be filled with grief and shame. But look here, I will pretend to be ill and say I cannot walk any more; then we can stay here till the dawn.' This he did. The others said, 'We will not go on either, but we will stay with you.' They sat there until the dawn, and in this way they did not upset the brother.[2]

Abba Antony said: 'Our life and death is with our neighbour. If we gain our brother, then we have gained God; but if we scandalize our brother then we have sinned against Christ.'

A hunter in the desert once saw Abba Antony enjoying himself with the brothers, and he was shocked. Wanting to show him that it was necessary sometimes to meet the needs of the brothers, the old man said to the hunter: 'Put an arrow in your bow and shoot it.' So he did. The old man then said: 'Shoot another arrow.' And he did so. Then the old man said: 'Shoot yet again.' But the hunter replied: 'If I bend my bow so much I will break it.' Then Antony said to him: 'It is the same with the work of God. If we stretch the brothers beyond their measure, they will soon break. Sometimes it is necessary to come down to meet their needs.'

Exercise 4.1: Creating your own cell

Most of us are not going to head off into the wilderness when we want some space and silence to be alone with God. Instead we may want to set aside some special place within our home as our 'cell', the place where we go when we want to spend some time apart. This isn't easy if you live in a small apartment or a house filled with other people and you have to be realistic about what is possible – Susanna Wesley (wife of the founding Methodist John) used the kitchen table with her apron over her head as her prayer-space. Here are some suggestions of how to set a space apart as your own cell which can be adapted to fit your particular circumstances.

(i)   Choose the room which has the least 'traffic' going through it and offers the best possibility of being both silent and undisturbed. If nowhere else is suitable, the bath can become a place of refuge and prayer!

(ii) Include an upright chair or, if you find it comfortable, a prayer stool or a cushion to sit cross-legged on. The important thing is to have somewhere to sit where you can keep your back straight and feel both relaxed and alert.

(iii) Have nearby an image of the holy. This could be a cross or an icon or something more abstract, whatever speaks to you of God.

(iv) Include a reminder of the wider world. This might be flowers, a leaf or a shell to remind you of God's creation; or it could be a newspaper cutting or photo to remind you of God's other children. Alternatively, you could set up your cell so that you can look out on the world outside.

(v)   In order to set aside a special time as well as a special place, you may find it helps to light a candle or burn some incense while you pray.

(vi)   If there is space, keep a small table close by to hold your Bible, or your current spiritual reading, a prayer journal and also a selection of drawing materials in case you feel like expressing your prayer through art.

(vii) Let people know that while you are in your cell you are, if possible, not to be disturbed.

Contemporary wildernesses

Not all wildernesses are picturesque stretches of unspoilt forest or desert. Indeed, the very fact that such places are pleasing to our eyes – full of beauty rather than threat – mean that they may not best represent what wilderness meant in the time of the Desert Fathers and Mothers. These spiritual seekers were not intending to commune with nature in its virgin state but to wrestle with demons and encounter God in a place which was challenging and inhospitable. They were not drawn by natural beauty but by the way the wilderness differed from everything that was considered civilized and comfortable. The Desert Fathers and Mothers sought out a place that was outside the civilized norm for human living. If we want to find such places today then we are more likely to go into our cities than to leave them behind.

In Vancouver there is an area known as the Downtown East Side. It is renowned as being one of the poorest and most deprived neighbourhoods in the whole of Canada. The people you see on the streets are nearly all down and out, walking along behind shopping trolleys piled high with cardboard boxes or carrying a blanket and a hat for begging with. There is a real drug problem here with crystal meth currently overtaking heroin as the street drug of choice and, of course, with alcohol also playing a large part. Compared to the rest of Vancouver the shops and apartment buildings are shabby and neglected, and it is an area that some people fear to walk through at night. The reason behind the problem has partly to do with Vancouver's climate – the fact that the winters are very mild compared to the rest of Canada makes it a good choice if you are living rough – and partly to do with city politics – better to have one identified area where all the problem people go, so that the rest of the city can feel safe and sparkling.

The Downtown East Side resembles a contemporary wilderness, a place where the safety net of society has failed and life is reduced to its bare necessities. It is not, for most of its residents, a wilderness that they have chosen but a wilderness where they have found themselves through the circumstances of a troubled life. They would not see it as a place where spiritual enlightenment is waiting round the corner but as the backdrop for their small daily triumphs and failures. Those who live elsewhere in the city see it as a problem area, uncivilized and threatening, where drugs fuel irrational and aggressive behaviour and where personal safety is not assured. It is a home of the modern demons of poverty and failure that haunt contemporary dreams as the devils of temptation did of old.

But still, like those more picturesque wildernesses, this is also a place of encounter with God. It can be a site for spiritual service, a place where we go to wash the feet of our brothers and sisters, and, in encountering them, find that we are also encountering God. And if this is the case for us who come as visitors from outside, surely it is no less a possibility for the residents. They may not see the streets as a spiritual place but they do indeed offer the possibility to encounter Christ in the stranger's face and to act as Christ for another human being. The wilderness may find ourselves at the end of our resources discovering a new source for strength, and a new sense of community with those around us. While the Downtown East Side is a source of anxiety for some it may be for others a place where they have discovered an accepting community and feel themselves to have achieved a degree of relative safety.

It is also true that not all wildernesses look threatening and poor. There is another form of contemporary wilderness which has nothing to do with material deprivation but all to do with spiritual stagnation and deep loneliness. This is the wilderness created by the affluent who feel the need to protect themselves and their possessions from the rest of the world. It is possible to feel yourself in a wilderness in the heart of a middle-class suburb or a prosperous gated community – in any place where relationships have broken down and isolation results. This is another human way of creating wilderness: not through poverty and neglect but through fear and competition and a failure of community. Many of us do not have to go far from our own front doors in order to find demons that need fighting and also, in moments of grace, to encounter the presence of God.

Exercise 4.2: Stations

One form of traditional ritual prayer in Catholic Christianity is the 'Stations of the Cross', during which an individual or group moves around the church stopping to pray at fourteen stations. These stations follow Christ's journey from his trial to his crucifixion, sometimes including a fifteenth – the resurrection.

This exercise[3] takes the idea of stations as places where you stop and think and pray and applies it to a different context – that of your local neighbourhood. The prayers can be used together as a mini pilgrimage for an individual or a group. Alternatively the separate prayers could be used as and when you find yourself at one of the stations.

(i)   Prayer at your front door: Stop as you step outside and look back at your front door. Give thanks for the security of your own home, hold in your heart the people who share it with you and remember before God all those who have no roof over their heads.

(ii)   Prayer in the street: As you walk along the street become conscious of those who share it with you: the other pedestrians, the drivers, the birds and dogs, those in a hurry, those dawdling along. Think about your own journey of faith: where is God calling you to walk? How are you being called to walk with others in your community?

(iii)   Prayer at a bus-stop or railway station: Be aware of others making a journey, of their different possible destinations, of the lives that touch and overlap. Pray for those whose journey at this time takes them through lonely and desolate places.

(iv)   Prayer at a school: Think about the energy and hope and vulnerability of childhood. Give thanks for good teachers and mentors and all those who encourage growth. Be aware of your own need both to learn and to play. Remember before God those children who are bereaved or abused.

(v)   Prayer at a hospital: Acknowledge the pain, anxiety and distress of those who are ill in mind or body. Remember by name any of your own friends and family who are sick and give thanks for those who care for them. Consider your own wounds and ask that you may be open to God's healing love.

(vi)   Prayer at a shop: Look at what is on sale. Consider the work that has gone in to providing these goods. Think of the workers, especially those who are not justly recompensed for their work. What are the things that you want? What is it that you need?

(vii)   Prayer at a welfare agency: Notice those who are waiting to be helped. Notice those who are helping them. What emotions do you see? What are your own emotions at the scene? How can you contribute to a more just and caring society?

(viii)   Prayer at the gutter: Notice what is thrown away and discarded. Think about the people that our society discards – refugees, the mentally ill, the unemployed. Who have you helped turn into a victim? Who have you helped release?

(ix)   Prayer at a place of entertainment: Bring to mind some of the things in your life that bring you joy, and give thanks for them. Remember the little things over the last week that have made you smile. Give thanks for our human ability to celebrate and to enjoy one another's company.

(x)   Prayer at an old people's home: Think of the older people who have influenced your own life journey. Consider your own stage of life and how you would like to move into the future.

(xi)   Prayer at an office block: Give thanks for all the ways in which your life has been fruitful. Be aware of the energy that flows into, and out from, creative and fulfilling work.

(xii) Prayer at a church: Take a moment to recollect that you, your neighbourhood and all its people are constantly in the presence of God. Remind yourself that there is no place so desolate or so affluent as to be outside God's loving care. Conclude with any prayers that have arisen from your stations and say the 'Our Father'.

The dark night

Not all wildernesses are geographical or even external. It is one of the strengths of Christian spirituality that it does not hesitate to engage with the interior wildernesses that often prove a tougher place to inhabit than their external counterparts. The saint most closely connected with these arid internal places is St John of the Cross, a Spanish monk and mystic of the sixteenth century, who is famous for coining the phrase 'the dark night of the soul'. John was born in 1542 into a poor family in Fontiveros, his father having been disinherited by his wealthy family after his marriage to a girl of lower social standing. John's father died when he was still a boy so he was obliged to try and help his mother support the family. They moved to Medina where he worked in the hospital as a nurse while also continuing his education at a Jesuit school. At the age of 21 he joined the Carmelites and was sent by them to study in Salamanca. Back in Medina he met St Theresa of Avila who was already involved in reforming the Carmelite order of nuns. John followed her in this work, extending it to the friars, and, in the process falling foul of the Church authorities. This led to John spending nine months in a small prison room until he managed to escape in August 1578. He spent the next years founding monasteries and acting as a spiritual director to Theresa's nuns. In the last years of his life he was again the subject of official displeasure being forced to move to one of the poorest monasteries and finally to the monastery of Ubeda where he died in 1591.

John's writings all date from during or after the period he spent in close confinement. While in prison he composed four poems, one, *The Spiritual Canticle*, having thirty-one stanzas. The poem 'Dark Night' was composed just after his escape in 1578. His prose works, unusually, are commentaries on the poems with the Commentary on the Dark Night being written in 1584. John's poems can be characterized as reflections of his own spiritual experience while the commentaries attempt to put that experience at the service of other Christians. He writes with honesty and insight about both the joys and the struggles of Christian discipleship; showing us a path that is both arduous and, ultimately, glorious in its final destination: unity with God.

This path involves two 'dark nights', the first a dark night of the senses and the second a dark night of the spirit – two 'little deaths' on the way to a greater life. The dark night of the senses is intended to allow us to focus on God and to love God without any lesser foci and lesser loves holding us back. One image he uses is of a bird being held back from flight by an anchor chain or even by a thread. The dark night of the senses is the time when we free ourselves of all other bonds in order to be open and attentive to God's love alone. At this stage of prayer what is needed is not extra effort on the part of the pray-er but, on the contrary, a relaxation into a passivity which allows God to do the work:

> At this time a person's own efforts are of no avail, but an obstacle to the interior peace and work God is producing in the spirit through that dryness of sense. Since this peace is something spiritual and delicate, its fruit is quiet, delicate, solitary, satisfying and peaceful, and far removed from all the

other gratifications of beginners which are very palpable and sensible.[4]

This dark night may sound daunting enough but it is only the first step on John's description of the spiritual journey. It is not sufficient that we let go of our attachments to things of lesser worth than God, we must also give up our attachment to our humanly created images of God. This is the dark night of the spirit when our religious certainties become uncertainties and we lose the experience of comfort and consolation in prayer. John is both describing something that has been a real part of his own spiritual journey and something that he believes all Christians need to experience before they can reach the highest degree of spiritual closeness to God. Both the night of the senses and the spirit are intended to set one free from the attachment to anything that is less than God – even if that is the images with which our limited human minds clothe God. Part of the spiritual journey is learning how far God is from being caught within our nets of finite words and sensations, as John says: 'beginners desire to feel God and taste Him as if he were comprehensible and accessible. This desire is a serious imperfection and, because it involves impurity of faith, opposed to God's way.'[5] Pure faith is trust in God that is based on love and wonder rather than on an assumed knowledge and sense of control.

The dark night is not an end in itself but a necessary stage of emptying in order that we can then be filled more completely with God's love and presence. This 'living flame of love', to use John's own phrase, is what the dark night is all about. Although the experience itself feels like a time of aridity – that your prayer is dry and empty and the reassuring sense of God's presence is gone – it is actually a time of spiritual growth and maturing: a sign of new life just around the corner. It is a pattern of spiritual development which echoes the founding story of Christianity itself: that full resurrection life only comes after the encounter with the depths in a death. Or, to put it another way, it teaches that death is not the end and definition of Christian life but that resurrection is.

Dark night experiences are not necessarily dramatic or one-offs. Most of us who are walking the spiritual way experience times when our prayer and spiritual life seems to be regressing rather than progressing and to be empty of the significance and sustenance that it had given us before. It may feel like we are walking through a long grey afternoon of the soul rather than something as profound as a dark night. It is reassuring to realize that such times may well be signs of our progress towards a greater degree of spiritual maturity rather than of our greater alienation from the things of God. Dark nights allow us to put away a relationship with a God who is made in our own image, or in images adopted from other people's spiritual experience, in favour of a relationship with the God who is beyond all our words and images.

It is important to make a distinction between a spiritual dark night and a psychological state of depression. St John of the Cross realized that the two might easily be confused, as both depression ('melancholia' in the language of his time) and a spiritual dark night leave one feeling dissatisfied, restless and just plain miserable. The difference lies in the desire, or lack of it, to continue to serve God. If the person is purely melancholic 'there are none of these desires to serve God that accompany the purgative dryness'; whereas if they are undergoing a true dark night, 'Even though in this purgative dryness the sensory part of the soul is very cast down, slack and feeble in its actions because of the little satisfaction it finds, the spirit is ready and strong.'[6] The dark night is not an easy place to be in but it is not to be identified with a depressive state but rather with a temporary place of purgation and loss that allows a transition to eventually take place.

Dark night feels like an interior wilderness as all our customary certainties and reference points are stripped away. But wilderness, as we have already seen with the Desert Fathers and Mothers, can often be a place of encounter with God. John's dark night is not an empty space, although it does involve emptying, nor a barren one, although it may feel so in comparison to the 'green pastures' of our earlier spiritual experience. Rather it can be seen as the 'steep and rugged pathway' that leads to the next level of our encounter with God. It is not something to fear as an obstacle that lies in our path, but something to endure – perhaps even welcome – as a way of gaining greater intimacy with the reality of God. Most importantly, it is a reminder that our subjective experience does not reflect the reality of God's presence in our life: when we are least aware of God she is as present, and as loving, as when we are most aware of her presence. The wild wilderness is as full of God's love as the most civilized city street.

Exercise 4.3: Our images of God

One of John's hopes for the dark night was that it would cleanse individuals of their inadequate images of God, and so allow the reality of God to draw closer to them. Before we reach a place in our spiritual journey where this is appropriate we need to recognize and acknowledge the images of God that help and hinder us in our prayer life now.

(i)   Find yourself a comfortable position in which you can stay still comfortably.

(ii)   Become conscious that you are, now as always, in the presence of God. Invite God to assist your journey towards God.

(iii)   Let yourself become aware of everything that arises in you in response to the word 'God'. These might include particular emotions or states of mind, other words (such as Lord, Father, Mother), or a visual image. Stay for a few minutes with whatever comes to you most vividly.

(iv)   Reflect on anything that you find particularly helpful about this response to God. Give thanks for this.

(v)   Reflect on anything that you find uncomfortable about this response to God. Open this up to God's healing.

(vi)   Offer your response to the God who is beyond the feelings, words and pictures.

(vii)   Close with the 'Our Father', a prayer that unites Christians wherever they are on their spiritual journey.

Questions for further reflection

(1) The Desert Fathers and Mothers show us an extreme reaction against the culture and society of their time. Do you think there is a need for a similar movement of rejection and retreat in the Church today? Would it be even possible, let alone desirable, for modern Christians to step aside from the overflow of information available in the world to find stability and focus in whatever would be the modern equivalent of a desert cell?

(2) The Desert Fathers and Mothers spoke often of fighting demons and avoiding the snares of the devil, continuing the language and imagery used throughout the New Testament. Do you believe that such language continues to have a place within contemporary Christian discourse? If so, how would you interpret it to have meaning within our current understanding of scientific and psychological truth?

(3) St John of the Cross is clear that the dark night of the soul is very different from a general depressive state. How would you discern this and differentiate between the two?

Notes

1. This and the following quotations are all taken from *In the Heart of the Desert: The Spirituality of the Desert Fathers and Mothers*, John Chryssavgis, Bloomington: World Wisdom, 2003.
2. From *The Sayings of the Desert Fathers: The Alphabetical Collection*, tr. Benedicta Ward, Kalamazoo: Cistercian Publications, 1975.
3. This exercise is strongly influenced by Simon Bailey's *Stations: Places for Pilgrims to Pray*, Sheffield: Cairns Publications, 1991.
4. *John of the Cross Selected Writings*, ed. Kieran Kavanagh O.C.D., New Jersey: Paulist Press, 1987, p.183.
5. *John of the Cross Selected Writings*, p.175.
6. *John of the Cross Selected Writings*, p.181.

Chapter 5

Body

For it was you who formed my inward parts;
you knit me together in my mother's womb.
I praise you, for I am fearfully and wonderfully made.
                                                    Psalm 139:13–14a

Spirituality, in many people's minds, is, almost by definition, uninterested in anything to do with the bodily or the material. It is, after all, *spirit*uality – concerned with things of the soul and the heavenly rather than with things of the body and the earthy. Indeed, not just unconcerned with body and earth but frequently believed to be in positive opposition to them. True spiritual success is seen to lie in an ability to set oneself apart from the passions and attachments that mark normal human life so that one is free to focus on higher, truer realities. This is not only true of some strands of Christian spirituality but also of strong schools within Hindu and Buddhist spiritual belief and practice.

In this chapter we will look at the place of the body and the bodily within spirituality; attending to the early ascetic traditions, the different meaning of body within the context of Eucharistic spirituality and the new place that is being found for the body within the understanding of liberation spiritualities. Part of this consideration will be some reflection of the roles that gender, sexuality and disability play in our spiritual lives. The whole chapter will be set within the context of a discussion of dualism, a philosophical worldview that has had a serious and long-lasting impact on Christian spirituality in a variety of different ways.

Dualism and spirituality

Dualism is a way of looking at the world which divides it into two camps defined in opposition to each other. It began in pre-Christian Greek philosophy and had a substantial influence on early writers of Christian theology. Dualism was, in effect, the unquestioned assumption that underlined the way that people understood themselves, their relationships to one another, the world around them and the divine above them: hierarchical language is very appropriate when discussing dualism.

The upper end of the dualistic system as adopted by Christianity was based on their understanding of the attributes of the divine. Their way of thinking went: God is the ultimate good, therefore everything that resembles the divine nature is superior to everything that does not. It is important to the understanding of the history of Christian spirituality to see which attributes they decided were God-like. These included: spirit (God is spirit), intellect (God is rational), heaven (where God dwells), changelessness (God is unchanging). At the other end of the spectrum were those attributes considered furthest from the divine nature: matter (God is not material), emotion (God is – to use the technical theological term 'impassible', i.e. God is not swayed by emotion), earth (where God does not dwell except temporarily in the person of Jesus Christ) and changeability (God does not change).

The spiritual journey was understood as a climb upwards. The starting point was the lower end of the spectrum among all that was earthy, emotional and changeable. This is where the human body is at home. The challenge was to move from this natural state to the other end of the spectrum where all that was most worthy, including God, was located. So in practice this meant favouring the needs of the soul over those of the body, attempting to put reason in control of the emotions, focusing on life after death rather than life before death and attempting to find detachment from all the passing things of this world in favour of the unchanging things of the world to come. A spirituality that taught the body was unimportant – or even a barrier to God – and that the soul was the only important part of a human being.

There was an interesting further corollary of this dualistic worldview which has to do with how it impacted on men and on women. Basically, men – and masculinity – were identified with the top end of the duality and women – and femininity – with the bottom end. This is partly due to women's role as birth-givers, which has been seen as linking us intrinsically with the physical messiness of life, and partly due to the power differential between the genders in earlier patriarchal societies which allowed men to define themselves favourably in opposition to women. So the spiritual journey was traditionally understood to be harder for women than for men – women had to step further away from their intrinsic nature to get close to God, while men were already some of the way there.

This gender imbalance is one of the troubling inheritances from dualism within Christian spirituality. It has been a long journey away from the concept that men are more naturally spiritual than women, and remnants of this way of thinking are still found in the arguments used by some opponents of the ordination of women to the priesthood. Indeed the whole emphasis within Roman Catholic spirituality on women's role as mothers continues our identification with our bodily nature. The other troubling inheritance is the belief that our soul/spirit/mind links us with the divine and our bodies link us with all that is not divine. Just as dualism has allowed the devaluing of women so dualism has allowed the devaluing of the bodily and the earthly. As shown, perhaps, by the ascetic spirituality which provides our next focus.

Ascetic spirituality

Ascetic spirituality has had something of a bad press of late. Ascetic spirituality is linked with all within traditional Christianity that is life-denying and anti-body. It is associated with saints who went in for strange physical self-deprivation: ascetic spirituality is seen as being all about wearing hair shirts, whipping oneself or refusing to eat anything other than the bread of the Eucharist. In some contemporary thinking it is an aberration of early and mediaeval Christianity which mistakenly embraced suffering as a spiritual good in itself. Ascetics failed to understand that created matter as well as eternal spirit could be embraced as a good and integral part of God's creative purposes.

Ascetic spirituality also scores badly on the contemporary chart of popular spirituality because it is associated with the concept of original sin that some Christians now question. Original sin, an early doctrine associated with St Augustine, teaches that all human beings are born tainted with sin and, therefore, separated from God. Part of the spiritual task, therefore, is to do anything you can to separate yourself from sin so that you can be united with God. Recently the doctrine of original blessing, made popular in the writings of Matthew Fox, has gained more ground. This teaches that all human beings are fundamentally linked to God and are a delight to God. The spiritual journey, therefore, is more like a walk in the park than a strenuous climb: we need to delight in ourselves, and one another, in order to become more like God.

But is there still some worth to be found within the ascetic tradition? The word 'ascetic' comes from the Greek word 'askesis' meaning 'training' or 'discipline', and this was the original intention and direction of ascetic spirituality. It was not an end in itself but a way of discipline which brought one closer to the kingdom of God: a way of allowing God into our life so as to 'make us truly alive', in words from the fourth-century Eucharistic prayer of Serapion of Thmuis.[1] This opening up to God did involve a degree of closing oneself off from some of the usual joys of human living. St Paul, for example, taught that due to the imminent coming of God's kingdom celibacy was preferable to the married life as this would allow one more time to focus on God and God's works. In a similar way, possessions and wealth were thought to be a distraction from God's calling and, in the early Church, were to be shared among all believers. Asceticism was a way of focusing the self on the things that were truly important in this life – and these were understood to be the things that would lead most directly into God's kingdom.

Ascetic spirituality became more directly connected with suffering during and following on from the times of official persecution and martyrdom of Christians. Martyrdom was seen as the highest achievement of a Christian, in which they imitated the voluntary death of Christ and so received automatic entry into heaven and the delight of God's blessed presence. The suffering involved was still not seen as an end in itself but a door into God's presence and a way of witnessing to the strength and passion of one's faith: the word 'martyr' means 'witness'. We have already talked in Chapter 4 about the way that the Desert Fathers and Mothers saw their move to the desert as a way both of imitating martyrdom in the retreat from worldly pleasures and also as a protest against a Christian way of life that was becoming more socially acceptable and comfortable: a witness to a more radical way of living out one's faith. Even at this stage, however, Christians were discouraged from indulging in extreme physical disciplines which were seen both as damaging to the body and, therefore, incapacitating the Christian from prayer and service, and as damaging to the soul in that they could lead to pride and excessive self-esteem.

Ascetical spirituality as a discipline gradually became closely identified with the eremitic or monastic life and the vows of poverty, chastity, obedience and stability that went with it. As the time of the martyrs faded into the past there was less emphasis on extreme austerities and more on the discipline of communal living with its stress on both obedience and charity. Christians still living in the world might be encouraged towards a simplicity of lifestyle but it was the religious brothers and sisters who were expected to be the true athletes and champions of austerity and spiritual achievement. Indeed, it was this seeming belittling of the spiritual possibilities of everyday married life that was one of Martin Luther's quarrels with the monastic system of his day.

Although extreme bodily discipline was not officially encouraged there were those who saw it as the best path into an experience of God's embrace. This was particularly true of some of the women mystics of the medieval and early modern periods. Women, of course, had an extra reason to seek bodily discipline: our bodies were seen as further from the divine than man's, as woman in general was less completely in the image of God than man was. One quote from Augustine is enough to illustrate this point: 'The woman together with the man is the image of God, so that the whole substance is one image. But when she is assigned as a helpmate, which pertains to her alone, she is not the image of God: however, in what pertains to man alone, is the image of God just as fully and completely as he is joined with the woman into one.'[2] In other words, man is always fully in the image of God but woman only when viewed together with man. This inspired women to work even harder than men at belittling the physical body in search of spiritual growth. Extreme ascetic practices included an emphasis on the control of all bodily appetites, with some women achieving spiritual notoriety by apparently refraining from all food except for the elements of the Holy Eucharist. In such extremes, ascetic spirituality did segue into a form of bodily punishment with the overt purpose of nourishing the soul at the body's expense.

One of the main arguments against ascetic spirituality is that it is often premised on the basic duality, outlined at the beginning of this chapter, in which the soul and the spiritual are valued while the body and the material are devalued. This opens the door to an acceptance of bodily abuse and suffering as of no account, or as positively beneficial on the Christian spiritual journey: a teaching that has contributed in the past to Church leaders counselling abused women to value their marital vows above their physical safety and wellbeing. This way of thinking should not have any place within contemporary Christian spirituality. This part of ascetic spirituality should be left within the covers of history books.

However, this is not to say that there is no contemporary value for ascetic spirituality at all. If it is seen in its original meaning of a form of discipline grounded on the gospel call to open, simple and charitable living then it can continue to inform and add rigour to many different spiritual paths. It can act as a counter to the contemporary tendency towards self-indulgence and consumerism, reminding us of where our priorities ought to be – and reminding us that all the choices and decisions we make about what we buy and what we eat have spiritual as well as physical and economic consequences. Ascetic spirituality at its best is a call to bring all of our life into our spiritual quest and that is a lesson that we continue to need today.

Exercise 5.1: Self-discipline

Traditionally, Christians have been asked to either give something up in Lent or to take on an extra charitable or spiritual practice. Both the giving up and the taking up are ways of minimizing the busy clutter of our lives in order to focus on what is most important: our relationship with God and with God's people.

For this spiritual exercise you are invited to make an inventory of how you spend your time. Consider first an average day, and then an average week, seeing how much time you devote to work, to leisure, to caring for others, to caring for yourself, to watching TV, to reading, to sleep and to prayer. See if any of these elements is out of balance – receiving an undue amount of your time or too little. Consider how this might be changed – discussing the changes with any other people they might involve or impact on. Resolve to try the change for a limited period and reflect on any difference it makes in how you feel physically, spiritually and emotionally.

Liberation spirituality and the bodies of the poor

Liberation Theology is a movement which first took root in the Roman Catholic Church in Latin America in the 1960s and 70s, and which has since then influenced a great deal of theological thinking across the world and across denominations. It is a movement which is grounded in the need to take bodies very seriously, focusing as it does on the needs of the poor and the oppressed, and on the Christian calling to make a difference to this world rather than to wait for all injustice to be put right in the next. This is how Gustavo Gutierrez, one of the founding fathers of Liberation Theology, explains its understanding of Christian discipleship:

> To be a disciple of Jesus is to make his Messianic practice our own. Our discipleship is our appropriation of his message of life, his love for the poor, his denunciation of injustice, his sharing of bread, his hope for resurrection. The Christian community, the ecclesia, is made up of those who take up that messianic practice of Jesus and use it to create social relation ships of a community of brothers and sisters, and thereby accept the gift of being children of the Father. Messianic practice is the proclamation of the kingdom of God and the transformation of the historical conditions of the poor. It is the word of life, backed up by the deed of deliverance.[3]

It is a this-wordly theology, and for some critics it has appeared to be more of a Marxist political movement than a true flowering of Christian thought and, with more justice, it has often been seen as a theology of activism which is disinclined to take spirituality as seriously as it should.

This, however, does Liberation Theology an injustice. It does have a profound spirituality of its own, one which argues against the dualism that has been at the heart of much Christian understanding of both prayer and of the body itself and which argues for the involvement of the whole person in the spiritual quest. One of the best words to describe it would be 'incarnational': a spirituality which honours the presence of Christ in every human being, and which has as a prime goal the enabling of a system of just living which will allow each individual the freedom to discover, live out and celebrate the divine image within. This will, of necessity, be a spirituality which is focused outwards as well as inwards but it will also be one that assures Liberation Theology of remaining a Christian movement with political and social consequences rather than being a political and social movement with only a nodding acquaintance with Christian faith.

Liberation spirituality has as its goal the inspiring of right behaviour, known as 'ortho-praxis', rather than right belief, 'orthodoxy'. It will be seen elsewhere in this book, particularly in Chapter 7 on Mystery, that this is not the goal for liberation spirituality alone: it is a prevalent theme among Christian spiritual writers that our spiritual journeys are not made primarily for our own benefit but for the benefit of all God's world. While this is sometimes spiritualized – the good of others being seen as their strengthening in right belief so that their ultimate salvation is assured – for liberation spirituality it remains profoundly incarnational – the good of others is their flourishing in this world. It is an integral part of this spirituality, therefore, to work for a world where such flourishing is possible; and also to take the fate of the poorest members of society as the standard to judge whether change is happening for the better. Liberation Theology famously talks about God's 'preferential option for the poor', meaning that those in greatest need are most especially cared for by God, so liberation spirituality sees spiritual health as impossible without us also caring for the poor and working with them to improve their lives.

This 'working with them' is also central to liberation spirituality. Its characteristic practice is not by an individual but by a community, a group of committed companions working together to interpret scripture and theology so that they both make sense to, and also have a liberating impact on, people's lives today. Communities together work to see where the Spirit is at work in their lives and in their neighbourhood, and put themselves at the disposal of the Spirit to continue this work – in many places of the world at great personal risk to themselves. Communities discover the meaning of biblical stories within their own context, and are motivated by this to live out the truth that these stories contain. Archbishop Oscar Romero, martyred while celebrating mass on 24 March 1980, explained this aspect of liberation spirituality in one of his homilies in October 1978:

A community is a group of men and women

who have found the truth in Christ and in his gospel,

and who follow the truth

and join together to follow it more strongly.

It is not just an individual conversion,

but a community conversion.

It is a family that believes,

a group that accepts God.

In the group, each one finds that the brother or sister

is a source of strength

and that in moments of weakness they help one another

and, by loving one another and believing,

they give light and example.

The preacher no longer needs to preach,

for there are Christians who preach by their own lives.[4]

This is where liberation spirituality finds the strength for liberating praxis: in a communal working out of God's calling, in a shared understanding of the meaning of the Bible and especially of Jesus' incarnational mission, and in a conviction that in working for change in the world we are walking in the footsteps of Christ and growing into the divine likeness. This is the spiritual calling of the Church as seen by liberation spirituality. It is fitting to end with more words of Archbishop Romero, which express this most eloquently:

> *Christ became a man of his people and his time:*
>
> *He lived as a Jew,*
>
> *he worked as a labourer of Nazareth,*
>
> *and since then he continues to become incarnate*
>
> *in everyone.*
>
> *If many have distanced themselves from the church,*
>
> *it is precisely because the church has somewhat*
>
> *estranged itself from humanity.*
>
> *But a church that can feel as its own all that is human,*
>
> *and wants to incarnate the pain,*
>
> *the hope,*
>
> *the affliction of all who suffer and feel joy,*
>
> *such a church will be Christ loved and awaited,*
>
> *Christ present.*
>
> *And that depends on us. (3 December 1978)[5]*

Exercise 5.2: Do something

The one spiritual exercise to recommend as a way in to liberation spirituality, is to get out there and get involved where the needs are greatest. Live out your Christian understanding of God's love for all people, and Christ's presence among the marginalized, by doing at least one of the following: volunteering, joining a pressure group for change, supporting a political party which you feel will accomplish beneficial change, writing letters for Amnesty International, committing to support a charity working with those in the underclass in your home country or abroad. In order to help you decide which of these activities to undertake you may find it helpful to undertake the liberation spirituality method of reflecting on a scriptural story within your own particular context – and if you can do this with a group of local people even better. The Parable of the Good Samaritan would be an excellent place to start.

Feminist spirituality as embodied spirituality

Liberation spirituality focuses on the bodies of the poor as a place of need and a challenge to live lives which properly follow the calling and example of Christ. Feminist spirituality also focuses on the body but in a rather different way. It is as keen as Liberation Theology to move away from a classic system of dualism, but rather than concentrating on poverty as a spur to spiritual reflection and action it focuses on gender, and what it means to live out our spirituality as embodied women and men. In particular it has explored the religious experiences of women and brought these both into its understanding of who we are as human beings created in God's image, and of who this God is whose image we bear. And just like liberation spirituality it is deeply incarnational, stressing God's immanence rather than God's transcendence: in other words, emphasizing that we encounter God in one another and in the physical world she created.

Feminist spirituality takes bodies seriously in a number of ways. Rather than seeing us as souls who are trapped in bodies which somehow separate us from the God who created us, Christian feminist spirituality sees us as primarily bodily creatures, created by God to rejoice in our physicality and in the physical world of which we are part. We do not *have* a body, we *are* a body, and any spirituality which does not address this part of our nature is seen as anaemic and inadequate to the task of enabling us to live into the image of a God who chose incarnation as the primary way to reveal her nature. As embodied creatures on a communal spiritual journey we are called to consider the way that our bodies allow us to relate to others: whether our gender or colour gives us privilege and power, how our appetites and perceived needs impact on the resources of the natural world and other people and whether our physical actions reach out to others in hospitable love or close ourselves off in fearful seclusion.

There are certain dangers inherent in focusing on our bodies in the way that feminist spirituality does. One of the most persistent is the risk of turning biology into destiny through imagining that there are particular spiritual roles which only men or only women can live out: something that the Church has been disappointingly keen to do for most of its life and something which most writers on feminist spirituality are very keen to avoid. An essential aspect of Christian feminist spirituality is the equal value to be placed on women and men, both created in God's image and both called to live as Christ to the world through the in-dwelling grace of the Holy Spirit. Men are no more called than women to be leaders and thinkers, women are no more called than men to be carers and healers: both are called by God to develop both hearts and minds and to contribute fully to the world.

So what does it mean to have a bodily spirituality, if it doesn't mean that our bodies dictate who we should be? Partly it means that, like liberation spirituality, we keep a this-worldly focus and see spirituality as properly concerned with the physical wellbeing and flourishing of all people, and of the earth, and not majorly focused on thoughts of our life after death.[6] It also means finding language and imagery for God which reflects the reality that women as well as men are created in God's image. Feminist spirituality aims to provide women with ways that they can see themselves in the divine and, therefore, discover a spirituality which allows them to explore their embodied reality rather than ignoring it. This means more than replacing 'Father' with 'Mother', it involves finding many female images which speak of who God is – as these verses from a hymn by Kathy Galloway of the Iona Community shows:

She comes with mother's kindnesses

And bends to touch and heal.

She gives her heart away in love

For those who cannot feel.

She comes with lover's tenderness

To answer love's appeal,

She gives her body with her heart

To make her passion real.

She comes with worker's faithfulness

To sow and reap and spin.

She bends her back in common task

To gather harvest in.

She comes with sister's carefulness,

Strong to support and bind,

Her voice will speak for justice' sake,

And peace is in her mind.[7]

This use of language and imagery can be very freeing for women who have thought of themselves as second class spiritual citizens, though, of course, there continue to be many women who are comfortable with male language and imagery. But, even though female imagery, and referring to God as 'she' as well as 'he', may discomfort some it is still a crucial step in ensuring that we understand God as beyond gender and do not fall into the habit of thinking of God as an old man in the sky.

Feminist spirituality calls on us to bring all of who we are into our relationship with God: not to leave out our physical reality and focus only on our soul. This plays out into an understanding of prayer as being something which can be physical as well as mental in its expression. We can listen to our bodies to discover places in ourselves that need healing, whether physical, emotional or spiritual, and use our bodies to express whatever it is that we feel most in need of communicating to God. This form of prayer should not feel alien as it is already something we experience in our worshiping lives: sitting, standing, kneeling, maybe making the sign of the cross or genuflecting or lifting out arms in praise – all these are ways of bringing our bodies into our relationship with God. Feminist prayer just invites us to include some of this experience in our own personal prayer lives so that we live our spirituality as fully embodied humans, valuing our physicality as well as our intellect and spirit, and living into the declaration made in Genesis 1:31, 'God saw everything that he had made, and indeed, it was very good.'

Exercise 5.3: Praying with the body

This is a prayer of praise and self-offering expressed by gesture rather than by words. If you are unable to stand comfortably the same gestures can be performed sitting down.

(i)   Find a space where you have enough room to move and enough privacy to do so un-self-consciously.

(ii)   Begin by standing, or crouching if you feel comfortable, with your head bent and your hands clasped tight in front of your chest. Pause like this and register how it feels.

(iii)   Slowly straighten your body, and then raise your head to gaze straight ahead. Keep your hands still clasped in front of your chest.

(iv)   Slowly tilt your head upwards, at the same time opening and raising your arms, and opening your hands if they have been closed, in a gesture of openness and praise. Stay like this for a few moments seeing how it feels.

(v)   Now bring your arms down with your hands open, palms uppermost, in front of your chest. Allow yourself to accept whatever you feel God is putting in your open hands.

(vi)   Close your hands in the classic 'hands together' gesture of prayer and bow to God to close this movement of prayer.

(vii)   You may find it helpful to do this exercise more than once so that the gestures become more natural to you and require less thought to remember.

(viii) You may also want to journal about your experience – but try to reflect on how it felt in your body more than what you thought about it in your head.

Eucharistic spirituality and the Body of Christ

In a perfect segue from talking about one understanding of body to another, Elizabeth Stuart, a British feminist theologian, speaks of the sacrament of the Eucharist in this way: 'Christ's body is transposed into the multi-gendered, multi-ethical and multi-cultured body of the Church. We are Christ.'[8] The Eucharist, and understandings of the Church as the body of Christ, have been central to Christian self-understanding since the earliest days and this section will look at their continuing contribution to our spiritual lives today.

In the research for my first book I spent time talking with white working-class church-going women in the east end of Newcastle-upon-Tyne about what kept them coming to church through the years and what it was that they most valued about the experience. Their answers fell into two main categories: those who most valued the sense of fellowship they received and those who found the moment of communion a spiritually uplifting experience week after week. Here is a comment typical of the group valuing fellowship:

> What keeps me part of it is the fellowship, and I suppose it's been feeling part of a family. That there are people you've grown together, you're on a journey together and you become used to them. I think there's a bond of love there, and that's what keeps me going.[9]

and another woman speaking of the moment of receiving communion:

> You know you hear people saying, 'Well, there's God inside everybody?' Well, I know there is without even receiving, but you actually, when you receive, you get that, that warmth and glow that gives you strength. Lovely. I love it.[10]

Although neither of these women would think of themselves as theologians, or have the technical language of scholarly theology, they have each deeply understood something of what is meant when we talk about the Eucharist and the body of Christ: that we somehow are made into one body with Christ as the head and that we mysteriously receive Christ's body through the experience of Eucharist.

There are many different ways of understanding this 'real presence' of Christ in the Eucharist, from the transubstantiation of the elements of bread and wine to the fact that Christ promised to be present whenever two or three are gathered in his name. The technicalities are not crucial from the point of view of what we experience spiritually in the service. More important from this aspect is the belief that Christ is present with us in this worship, offering himself to us and inviting us into table fellowship with the Trinity. We are invited to a foretaste of the heavenly banquet when there will be true communion between all people, and between all people and their divine creator. Christians across the ages and throughout the world have found sharing the Eucharist together to be one of the most profound ways of being fed with God's grace and one of the most fruitful schools for learning how to become Christ-like.

In my theology I am comfortable to speak about receiving Christ's body in the elements of bread and wine: seeing them as still 'just' bread and wine but also as imbued with the divine presence, in the same way that a piece of paper is still a piece of paper but is also much more when it carries a person's last will and testament. In the beautiful words from one of the Iona liturgies: 'Christ has put his life in our hands', to which the only response is 'Now we put our lives in his.' It is the most characteristic act of Christian worship that we eat together and, in this eating, receive God into our very selves as we chew bread and sip wine. These two elements are wonderfully symbolic of both the ordinariness of life – the daily bread of everyday existence – and the extremes of life – the strong wine of joyful celebration and of searing tragedy being caught up into and transformed by God's grace at work within us.

It is not only the bread and the wine that are changed by our sharing of the Eucharist together: we are also changed. Through the Eucharist what happens to the bread and wine reflects what also happens to us. Bread is taken, blessed, broken and shared. We also can be taken – accepted by God as a friend and fellow worker, blessed – assured of God's loving-kindness and empowered to grow in God's Spirit, broken – opened up to God, not held tightly in our own control and shared – sent out to be Christ-like in love and service to the world. Communal and individual transformation are both to be looked for and expected through our participation in the offering, which always includes self-offering, of the Eucharist.

This transformation is our promised growing into the body of Christ. From the writings of St Paul onwards there has been an understanding that the Church somehow continues to incarnate God on earth: 'For just as the body is one and has many members, and all the members of the body, though many, are one body, so it is with Christ. For in the one Spirit we were all baptized into one body – Jews or Greeks, slaves or free – and we were all made to drink of one

Spirit' (1 Corinthians 12:12–13). This remains the Church's calling despite the many ways in which it has, and continues, to fall short of being the presence of Christ in the world. Together, for it is too much for any of us to accomplish alone, we are to continue to do the work that Christ began; not through our own abilities but through God's Spirit living within us, and always looking to Christ as our head.

The path to God's door in Christian spirituality is always one that is both unique to ourselves and yet also walked in community. As well as leading us to better understand, and better embody, the image of God within us that is our gift in creation, our Christian spiritual journey also leads us to become part of a larger body; one that exists across continents as well as across centuries and is renewed at each celebration of the Eucharist. All our bodies have worth and significance because all our bodies are incorporated within the Body of Christ; whether we are healthy or sick, presently able-bodied or living with disabilities, male, female, straight or gay we are all part of one great body which unites us with one another and with Christ our head. Both because it is an acknowledgement of this reality and because it allows us to live into this reality, celebrating the Eucharist together is a central and uniquely valuable Christian spiritual practice. The Eucharist affirms our bodily nature, feeds and strengthens us for our spiritual searching as well as for our active service and brings us together as the Body of Christ for the world today.

Exercise 5.4: Praying into the Eucharist

Eucharistic spirituality is, by definition, only truly experienced by taking part in a Eucharist. In most churches this is restricted to those who have been baptized, though a few churches do have a completely 'open table' where anyone who feels called to the love of God revealed in Christ can receive.

These are three prayers/poems one of which you might find helpful to reflect on before you next take communion:

Love bade me welcome; yet my soul drew back,
   Guilty of dust and sin.
But quick-eyed Love, observing me grow slack
   From my first entrance in,
Drew nearer to me, sweetly questioning
   If I lack'd anything.
'A guest,' I answer'd, 'worthy to be here:'
   Love said, 'You shall be he.'
'I, the unkind, ungrateful? Ah, my dear,
   I cannot look on Thee.'
Love took my hand and smiling did reply,
   'Who made the eyes but I?'
'Truth, Lord; but I have marr'd them: let my shame
   Go where it doth deserve.'
'And know you not,' says Love, 'Who bore the blame?'
   'My dear, then I will serve.'
'You must sit down,' says Love, 'and taste my meat.'
   So I did sit and eat.

George Herbert[11]

That which is Christ like within us
shall be crucified.
It shall suffer and be broken.
And that which is Christ like within us
shall rise up.
It shall love and create.

Michael Leunig[12]

Soul of Christ, sanctify me
Body of Christ, save me
Blood of Christ, inebriate me
Water from the side of Christ, wash me
Passion of Christ, strengthen me
O good Jesus, hear me

Within Thy wounds hide me
Separated from Thee let me never be
From the malicious enemy defend me
In the hour of my death call me
And bid me come unto Thee
That I may praise Thee with Thy saints
Forever and ever
Amen.

Anon. traditional

Questions for further reflection

(1) Asceticism is not a fashionable concept within Christian spirituality today, being identified with a theological emphasis on human sinfulness that can be seen as devaluing both divine grace and the original goodness of all created beings. Do you think this is a fair characterization of asceticism within the Christian tradition? Are there aspects of asceticism that you believe it would be detrimental for the Church to lose?

(2) Liberation spirituality has come under severe criticism, especially within the Roman Catholic hierarchy, for ditching the metaphysical in favour of the political and so losing the whole point of Christian theology and spirituality. Do you see there being any truth in this accusation, or does it miss the point of what liberation spirituality is trying to achieve? Or is the fact that liberation spirituality is 'trying to achieve' something a theological mistake in itself, in which human effort replaces divine activity?

(3) Feminist theology and feminist spirituality both like to challenge accepted assumptions within the life of the Church, especially around the valuation of women and men and of this world and the next – even to the extent of sometimes denying the existence of the last. Do you think this means they are losing a concept that is essential to the Christian faith, and to the practice of Christian spirituality?

Notes

1. Quoted from Rosemary Rader's article on Asceticism in *A Dictionary of Christian Spirituality*, ed. Gordon S. Wakefield, London: SCM Press, 1986, pp 24–8.
2. Augustine, *De Trinitate*, 12.7.10.
3. Gustavo Gutiérrez, *The Power of the Poor in History (La fuerza histórica de los pobres: selección de trabajos*, 1979), tr. Robert R. Barr, Maryknoll, NY: Orbis Books, 1983, p.96.
4. Oscar Romero, *The Violence of Love*, tr. James R. Brockman S.J., Maryknoll, NY: Orbis Books, 2004, p.111.
5. *The Violence of Love*, p.116.
6. There are indeed some Christian feminist theologians who believe that our existence is entirely embodied, and God is only to be known in this world – for example, Grace Jantzen's *Becoming Divine: Towards a Feminist Philosophy of Religion* (Bloomington: Indiana University Press, 1998) express this view.
7. In *Celebrating Women*, eds. Hannah Ward, Jennifer Wild, Janet Morley, Harrisburg: Morehouse Publishing Co., 1995, p.130.
8. Elizabeth Stuart, 'Exploding Mystery: Feminist Theology and the Sacramental' in *Embodying Feminist Liberation Theologies*, ed. Beverley Clack, London: Continuum, 2004, p.232
9. Ellen Clark King, *Theology By Heart: Women, the Church and God*, Peterborough: Epworth Press, 2004, p.142.
10. Ellen Clark-King, *Theology By Heart: Women, the Church and God*, p.141.
11. From *The Complete English Poems of George Herbert*, ed. John Tobin, London: Penguin Classics, 2005, p.178.
12. From Michael Leunig's *Common Prayer Collection*, Victoria: Collins Dove, 1993. The book has no page numbers.

Chapter 6

Desire

My beloved speaks and says to me:
'Arise, my love, my fair one,
and come away;
for now the winter is past,
the rain is over and gone.
The flowers appear on the earth;
the time of singing has come,
and the voice of the turtle-dove
is heard in our land.

Song of Solomon 2:10–13

There has always been a strand within Christian spirituality that shies away from desire: that reveres detachment and the intellectual pursuit of God and looks down on any involvement of the emotions within the pursuit of the divine. This is not something that we only find in older writings but also in the way that some Christians choose to live out their faith today. Such an attitude was there in the Puritans of the seventeenth century who found even the celebrating of Christian feasts such as Christmas unacceptable for its potential to arouse passionate feeling and jollity – which could not accompany true piety. Such an attitude is with us today in sections of the Church which focus almost exclusively on correct belief and strict self-control so that all our emotional impulses are brought under the direction of our intellect and our understanding of the faith.

These spiritual understandings contain great richness for some people, but there have also always been others within the Church who have brought their emotional intensity into their prayer and into their whole relationship with God. Sometimes their intensity has caused concern in the hierarchy of the Church because it has seemed to be beyond the control of Church doctrine and structures; sometimes seeming beyond the control of the individuals themselves. Among those who came under suspicion in this way is Mechthild of Magdeburg, a thirteenth-century continental mystic who was a member of the Beguine order, and who will be the first writer whose passionate spirituality and whose attitude to desire we will explore.

The second writer is very different – and a far more respectable member of the Church of his age. This is Ignatius of Loyola, the sixteenth-century founder of the Jesuit order, who invited his followers to understand their desires as a way to discover how and where God was at work in their lives. The chapter will end with a discussion of the way that desire finds a place within the writings of contemporary feminist liturgists, and how differently gendered language for God can open up the possibility of new understandings of our relationship with the divine.

Sensual spirituality

There are a number of spiritual writers within the Christian tradition that we could look to for a way of integrating desire and spirituality. These are often, though not exclusively women: Hadewijch, Hildegard of Bingen, Bernard of Clairvaux, Gertrude the Great and Catherine of Siena are some of the names which spring immediately to mind. They are characteristic of a form of spirituality known as 'bridal mysticism' where the soul and God are seen as bound together in a marriage of mystical intimacy and delight. The biblical starting point for this imagery is the Song of Solomon, whose love poetry has long been interpreted as referring to the relationship between a loving bridegroom God and a beloved bridal soul. The spiritual writer on whom we will focus is Mechthild of Magdeburg, whose book *The Flowing Light of the Godhead* is a great source for exploring the place of desire in our lives of prayer.

Mechthild lived in the thirteenth century in the Low Countries and was a member of a religious group known as the Beguines. This was a movement of women who wanted to live a religious life but didn't want to be part of a formal convent. They took vows committing themselves to poverty, chastity and the imitation of the life of Christ through service to the poor, but these vows did not have to be life-long. It was possible to spend some time as a Beguine and then embrace a more conventional married life. The Beguines usually formed small communities in the newly emerging urban centres and supported themselves by their own work rather than through the charity of others. Their uncloistered life brought them under suspicion from the Church officials, and the Pope eventually forced them into more traditional convent living. There was something threatening to the society, and the Church, of the time about women who lived under their own authority rather than being controlled either by Church structures or by a father or husband. Indeed the Beguines also came under suspicion for their theology: Marguerite Porete, a Beguine spiritual writer and near-contemporary of Mechthild, was burned at the stake as a heretic in 1310.

Mechthild herself knew that living her chosen form of life and daring to write about her spirituality made her vulnerable to accusations of heresy. Like many other women who had a role that could be seen as usurping a male prerogative she was careful to emphasize her own humility and submission to authority. Indeed, she claimed that the reason God gifted her with insight was due to her very position as a simple, unlearned woman. She writes that God says to her: 'I always sought out the lowest, most insignificant and most unknown … because the course of my Holy Spirit flows by nature downhill.'[1] This justifies, to herself if not to all the authorities, her writing of *The Flowing Light of the Godhead*, which is an extended love poem from Mechthild to God. It is a lengthy book, with many different moods reflected in its pages – unsurprisingly as Mechthild started writing it in about 1250 and continued after her enforced move to a Cistercian Convent in about 1270.

The imagery that Mechthild uses for her spiritual journey is diverse: there are sections which focus on the soul as a traveller in the wilderness, on the soul as a young child being caught up into the ranks of heavenly beings; and there are also practical sections which both take to task Church leaders for not living up to their calling and which also reflect on the earthly necessities for living a holy life: 'no hungry priest has ever sung beautifully, and no hungry man can study deeply'.[2] But the imagery that she is most known for, and which most characterizes her writing, is that of spiritual union with God understood through the passion and intimacy of sexual desire and union. Here is a passage from Book 1 which illustrates her imagery:

'Lord, now I am a naked soul

And you in yourself are a well-adorned God.

Our shared lot is eternal life

Without death.'

Then a blessed stillness

That both desire comes over them.

He surrenders himself to her,

And she surrenders herself to him.

What happens to her then – she knows –

And that is fine with me.

But this cannot last long.

When two lovers meet secretly,

They must often part from one another inseparably.[3]

There are a number of key points in this short passage which help us understand Mechthild's spiritual understanding. First, the classic definition of the soul as female and of God as male[4] which is the starting point for bridal imagery within the Christian tradition. This may be one reason why this imagery seems to come more naturally to female mystics, although it is also found in the writings of some men: notably Bernard of Clairvaux. Secondly, and very characteristic of Mechthild, the desire between the soul and God is a mutual attraction: God longs for union with the soul as well as the soul longing for union with God. Mechthild's understanding of our relationship with God was based on her theology of the creation, in which the Trinity creates humanity out of the desire to love and to be loved, so establishing a mutual longing for relationship which draws God and human souls into union. Thirdly, such blissful union is only ever a transitory experience in this life – God and the soul must part so that the soul can continue its bodily existence and the work which it has to do on earth. Permanent union is only to be experienced after death, which is why Mechthild looks forward to the day when she 'might die of love in love.'[5]

Although the language that Mechthild uses can seem extreme and foreign to us today – we seldom talk about 'entwining our limbs with God' when we think about our own prayer experiences – the spiritual truth that she expresses is still deeply relevant and a valued part of our Christian spiritual heritage. The sensual imagery is there to try to speak of the unspeakable as part of the constant struggle mystics have to share their understandings with the rest of us. Its point is that God and humanity are bonded together by a love so intense and intimate that sexual union is the only human experience passionate enough to provide a mirror for the divine relationship. And the longing for fulfilment of this relationship in loving union is not just one-way: God longs for us just as we long for God.

Desire for Mechthild is the natural way to speak of a spirituality which brings the emotions as well as the intellect into our relationship with God. Desire is not something to be afraid of or to be rigorously controlled, but instead to be embraced as the energy for our own spiritual quest. The point of it is not to experience mystical visions and joys but to bring us into communion with God and so to be infused with the humility and love and acceptance of suffering service that is seen most clearly in Jesus Christ. Desire and love help us to value the divine image in which we are made, and to grow into this image as we become more like that which we love. In the words of Mecthild herself: 'O blessed Love, / This has always been your task, and still is: / To bind together God and the human soul. / That shall be your task forever.'[6]

Exercise 6.1: Bringing desire into prayer

(i)   Read the Song of Solomon, travelling lightly over passages which seem strange to you and focusing on words and verses which appeal.

(ii) Listen, without judgment, to the feelings that the book arouses in you: these might be of joy, of amusement, of discomfort, of desire – or something else entirely.

(iii) Return to 8:6–7 and recall times when these words have had resonance with your own life, or times when you wish they would have been true for you.

(iv) Remembering how you have experienced love in your own life, write a love poem to God, or draw or make something that expresses your love for God.

(v)   Offer all you have experienced in this exercise to God, asking that it may lead you into deeper intimacy with God so that you may love God more dearly, day by day.

Ignatian prayer

There is another strand of Christian spirituality which takes desire very seriously, but works with it in a very different way from Mechthild and other continental mystic women. This is the tradition handed on to the Jesuits by their founder St Ignatius of Loyola. The story of Ignatius' conversion from soldier to saint is worth telling here as it helps show how his ideas on desire developed. Ignatius, who lived from 1491 to 1556, was severely wounded in battle in 1521. During his lengthy convalescence he kept himself entertained by telling himself stories of the heroic and romantic deeds of hero knights, imagining himself in the same role. These stories might have led Ignatius back to the battlefield had they not been supplemented, and eventually supplanted, by stories of the heroic deeds of Christian saints and martyrs. It was as Ignatius began to imagine himself in these roles that he found a satisfaction greater than his earlier day-dreaming had provided and began to picture himself as, above all, a knight-companion of Christ. This imaginative absorption into different roles helped Ignatius to identify where his deepest desires lay and provided the motivation to begin to try and live them out.

Ignatius wanted to provide ways in which other Christians could experience a similar transformative journey, and preferably without the necessity of being seriously injured to motivate them. The way he came up with to enable this is a spiritual tool which still has great relevance, and wide use, today. This is the Spiritual Exercises, which invite the pray-er into a journey that will bring them both into touch with their own deepest desires and also into a deeper commitment to Christ. Traditionally the Exercises are done over a four-week retreat, with the retreatant being carefully guided by a spiritual director. However it is also possible to do the exercises in the midst of everyday life, a form known as the 19th Annotation, which makes them more available for many working people. They still call for close guidance from a spiritual director, and for a serious time commitment of about an hour a day, but are capable of being adapted to many different daily routines.

The exercises are divided into four 'weeks' – the name coming from the original month long retreat – and they centre around Ignatius' 'Principle and Foundation', which could be called his definition of Christian spirituality:

Human beings are created to praise, reverence, and serve God our Lord, and by means of doing this to save their souls. The other things on the face of the earth are created for human beings, to help them in the pursuit of the end for which they are created. From this it follows that we ought to use these things to the extent that they help us toward our end, and free ourselves from them to the extent that they hinder us from it. To attain this it is necessary to make ourselves indifferent to all created things, in regard to everything which is left to our free will and not forbidden. Consequently, on our own part we ought not to seek health rather than sickness, wealth rather than poverty, honour rather than dishonour, a long life rather than a short one, and so on in all other matters. Rather we ought to desire and choose only that which is more conducive to the end for which we are created.

So the intention of the exercises is to let us uncover our true desires which, in Ignatius' view, are always going to lead us to God rather than away from God. They are meant to cut through the false desires and attachments that clutter up our lives and to lead us to a place where we can make a clear choice to be on God's side and to be a loyal follower of Christ.

The Exercises do this by leading us on a pilgrimage in company with Christ. The starting point is a conviction of God's great love for us, and a willingness to trust that love. In the first week the exercises focus on the ways that we have lost our companionship with God through sin: both our own wrong choices and the injustice and selfishness that is present throughout human society. The second week takes you through the birth, life and ministry of Jesus Christ as you imagine yourself into the biblical narrative and open yourself up to sharing the experiences of Christ. This sharing of experience continues in the third week as you journey deep into the experience of Christ's passion and death as we learn both of the depth of God's love and of the need not to be deterred by suffering and failure. The fourth and final week is an experience of the new life of resurrection and a commitment to living out this new life day by day. The hope is that by this stage of the exercises, the person taking them is able to truly pray Ignatius' prayer of commitment: 'Take, Lord, and receive all my liberty, my memory, my understanding and my entire will – all that I have and call my own. You have given it all to me. To you Lord I return it. Everything is yours, do with it what you will. Give me only your love and your grace. That is enough for me.'

The hope is that by the end of the exercises the person taking them will have realized that the path to true joy and fulfilment of their deepest desires lies through commitment to the way of Christ. Ignatius' own deep trust in God was mirrored by his understanding of human nature: that, although damaged by sin, we are creatures of the divine whose own deepest desires are still and always oriented towards God. It may take us a fair amount of work to uncover them from under the weight of all the worldly desires that tempt us away, but they are our own truest nature and the source of our own deepest happiness. At the deepest level of our souls there is no true division between God's desires for us and our own desires for ourselves: both are focused on us growing into the likeness of Christ as we find joy and completion in service and love.

Although all humans, in Ignatius' understanding, share the truest desire to become Christ-like – though not all can access this desire because of the damage they have done to themselves through sin – they also have individual ways in which they can best live this desire out. So, for some people, this would be through imitating the poverty of Christ in a religious vocation, for others through a life of love and service in the midst of a family and through activity in the world of work. Ignatius would quite possibly have been happy to echo the words of Frederick Buechner from the 1970s: 'The place God calls you to is the place where your deep gladness and the world's deep hunger meet.'[7] Accessing our desires means finding the particular way in which we can reflect the beauty of Christ into the world around us: a way that will be both true to Christ and true to our own inherent nature and character.

The Exercises is not the only tool that Ignatius left to help people identify their own way of living out Christ in their particular circumstances. Another widely used spiritual instrument is the Examen, which will be the subject of the spiritual exercise at the end of this section. It is a form of prayer often used to end the day to look back on the moments of greatest joy and greatest sorrow: the times when there was a sense of peace or of being filled with life, and the times when there was disquiet, dissatisfaction and a feeling that life and energy were draining away. As well as looking back on a day the prayer can be used at the end of any significant period of time: a week, month or year or at the end of a particular project or stage of life. Used over time it is one of the most useful ways of getting in touch with what in our lives gives us most joy and life and brings us to a point where we can see where our own deepest desires and the needs of the world coincide.

Exercise 6.2: The Examen

(i) Find a comfortable position – usually with both feet flat on the floor and a straight back is best, so that you can sit still and at ease.

(ii) Take a couple of minutes just to allow your body to relax. Allow yourself to become present to this moment and to yourself.

(iii) Call to mind the presence of God with you, now as always. And ask that God will accompany you in your reflection: opening up to you what is life-affirming and God-breathed in your life and also showing you what is life-denying and in need of God's healing touch.

(iv) Now allow the day to play back in your mind. Allow the moments which you enjoyed, which you are thankful for, to come to consciousness – don't scrabble around desperately trying to remember every event, just wait and see what comes to the surface, no matter how apparently insignificant or ordinary.

(v)   Let yourself feel those moments again, revisit the experience, take time to relish it.

(vi)   Now allow the day to play back again. Allow the moments that you were least grateful for to come to the front of your mind. Times when you felt weary or drained, isolated or anxious. Don't judge your feelings, just stay with them for a moment and think about where the feeling came from, and where it took you.

(vii)   What from this day would you like to take forward into tomorrow – what feeling, or insight, or intention?

(viii) What from this day would you like to open up to God's healing?

(ix)   Now ask your loving God for the grace you most feel in need of for tomorrow. Peace, or insight, or forgiveness, or courage – whatever you most stand in need of.

(x)   Bring this time of reflection to a close by thanking God for accompanying you in this prayer and by saying the Lord's Prayer or the words of the Grace.

Desire and feminist prayer

The title of one of the best books of feminist liturgy from the Anglican tradition, by the English poet and liturgist Janet Morley, is *All Desires Known*.[8] The phrase comes from one of the classic Anglican prayers, that begins both the Book of Common Prayer Eucharist service and also many modern Anglican Eucharistic rites. In its original form it reads: 'Almighty God, unto whom all hearts be open, all desires known, and from whom no secrets are hid; Cleanse the thoughts of our hearts by the inspiration of thy Holy Spirit, that we may perfectly love thee, and worthily magnify thy holy Name; through Christ our Lord.' This prayer from the superb writer of liturgy, Thomas Cranmer, puts desire right into the forefront of our worship – desire may be something that needs to be cleansed by God but it is not something that can be ignored when we consciously bring our humanity into the presence of the divine.

Worship, at its most fundamental level, is about our response in love to the love that we receive from God: it is a bringing together of our individual longing for ultimate truth and meaning in a communal expression of praise, confession, intercession and of the mutual interdependence of all created beings. We desire God and we seek to express that desire through our prayers and hymns, through our psalms and canticles, and through the very act of coming together with other people who are seeking and desiring God in their lives too. It has always been an essential part of Christian spirituality, as we saw in the previous chapter, that it is something more than a lonely search of a lonely soul for a lonely God. Our spirituality is a communal as well as an individual experience and so needs to find adequate expression through the words that we use together in public worship as well as through the words, and silences, that we use privately in our personal relationship with the divine.

Feminist theologians and writers of spirituality have been some of the loudest voices pointing out that the language we have inherited for worship is not always adequate to express the deepest longings and desires of our hearts. It is true, of course, to say that ultimately no language is entirely up to that task, but there are ways that we can improve our liturgies to ensure that they do as good a job as is possible in our particular time and culture. This language need not necessarily be new and innovative: for some Roman Catholics the Latin mass, through its sense of continuity and mystery, allows them to speak the truth of who they are in worship, and the same is true for some Anglicans with the Book of Common Prayer and many Orthodox congregations who still use the language of their original homeland even if it is not the tongue they speak everyday.

However feminist theology has pointed out one place in which many worshippers find the expression of their identity and their desires blocked. This is in the exclusively male language that has traditionally been used to speak of God. This is felt by some, though by no means all, Christians to impede the expression of desire in two somewhat different ways. The most obvious, and most often voiced, is that exclusively male language for the divine makes it difficult for women to see themselves as being created in the image of God, and obscures their call to grow into the divine likeness. This vocation to become more like God is hard enough at the best of times – and, of course, entirely impossible without the grace of God at work within us – but it is made even more arduous when the God we are called to be like seems to be imaged only in the bodies and pronouns of our fathers and brothers rather than of ourselves, our sisters and mothers.

It is not only women who are short-changed by liturgical language that is resolutely and only male. It may hamper our God-given desire to become more like God, but it can also hamper men's ability to fall in love with God. This may seem at first glance an odd thing to suggest that men ought to do, but the whole tradition of the Song of Solomon and nuptial spirituality invites us to do just that. For some heterosexual male Christians the ability to speak of God in female terms is as liberating as it is for many Christian women.

In illustration of this I want to quote at length one of Janet Morley's psalms from *All Desires Known*. It is entitled 'I will praise God, my beloved':

I will praise God, my Beloved,

for she is altogether lovely.

Her presence satisfies my soul;

she fills my senses to overflowing so that I cannot speak.

Her touch brings me to life;

the warmth of her hands makes me wholly alive.

Her embrace nourishes me, body and spirit;

every part of my being responds to her touch.

The beauty of her face is more than I can bear;

in her gaze I drown.

When she looks upon me

I can withhold nothing;

when she asks for my love all my defences crumble;

my pride and my control are utterly dissolved.

O God I fear your terrible mercy;

I am afraid to surrender myself.

If I let go into the whirlpool of your love,

shall I survive the embrace?

If I fall into the strong currents of your desire,

shall I escape drowning?

But how shall I refuse my Beloved,

and how can I withdraw from the one my heart yearns for?

On the edge of your abyss I look down and tremble;

but I will not stand gazing for ever.

Even in chaos you will bear me up;

if the waters go over my head, you will still be holding me.

For the chaos is yours also,

and in the swirling of the mighty waters is your presence known.

If I trust her, surely her power will not fail me;

nor will she let me be utterly destroyed.

Though I lose all knowledge and all security,

yet will my God never forsake me;

but she will recreate me in her steadfast love,

so that I need not be afraid.

Then will I praise my Beloved among the people,

among those who seek to know God.[9]

I used this passionate and challenging psalm in a service in the Cambridge college where I was currently chaplain. To my surprise the member of the small congregation who was most moved by it wasn't one of the young women present but one of the young men. He explained that he had always felt a barrier to his ability to love God because, as a straight male engineer, it felt uncomfortable for him to use love language towards a God who always seemed to be implicitly male. Hearing God spoken of as a beloved female allowed him to find a new way to speak to God, and a more personally appropriate image of the source of all love.

The words that we use of God are always woefully inadequate, but limiting them to one gender does nothing to help either gender discover the depth and extent of their desire for God and God's desire for them. The possibility of uncovering new images for God which begin with the female rather than the male is one of the Holy Spirit's gifts to the Church in the twenty-first century.[10] Hopefully it will make public worship a space where our desire for God finds true expression as we bring all of our selves – body, mind, heart and spirit – into our praise, our confession, our intercession and our mutual support.

Exercise 6.3: Praying with female images of God

(i)   Before you settle into prayer choose one of the following texts to work with:
       Either Janet Morley's psalm 'God is my strong rock':

God is my strong rock in whom I trust,

And all my confidence I rest in her.

Deep in my mother's womb she knew me;

Before my limbs were formed she yearned for me.

Each of my movements she remembers with compassion,

And when I was still unseen, she did imagine me.

Her strength brought me forth into the light;

It was she who delivered me.

Hers were the hands that held me safe;

She cherished me upon my mother's breast.

When I stammer, she forms the words in my mouth,

And when I am silent, she has understood my thoughts.

If I shout and rage, she hears my plea and my uncertainty.

When I am afraid, she stays close to me,

And when I am full of terror she does not hide her face.

If I struggle against her, she will contain me,

And when I resist her, she will match my strength.

But if I am complacent, she confronts me;

When I cling to falsehood, she undermines my pride;

For she is jealous for my integrity,

And her longing is for nothing less than truth.

To all who are weak she shows compassion,

And those who are downtrodden she causes to rise.

But she will confound the arrogant at the height of their power,

And the oppressor she will throw to the ground;

The strategies of the hard-hearted she will utterly confute.

God pities the fallen, and I will love her;

She challenges the mighty, and I desire her with my whole heart.

God is the rock in whom I put my trust,

And all my meaning is contained in her;

For without God there is no security,

And apart from her there is no place of safety.[11]

Or Edwina Gateley's poem 'A Warm, Moist, Salty God':

Deep in the forest

I found my God

leaping through the trees,

spinning with the glancing sunlight,

caressing with the breeze.

There where the grasses

rose and fell

fanning the perfumed air,

I smelt her beauty,

elusive, free,

dancing everywhere.

Deep in the city

I found my God

weeping in the bar,

prowling beneath the glaring lights,

dodging speeding car.

There where the women

were pimped and raped,

cursing for a light,

I felt her presence,

fierce, deep,

sobbing in the night.

Deep in myself

I found my God

stirring in my guts,

quickening my middle-aged bones,

stilling all my buts.

There where my spirit

had slumbered long,

numbed into a trance,

A moist, warm, salty God

arose,

and beckoned me to Dance.[12]

(ii)   Find yourself a space where you can be comfortable and still
         for a few minutes.

(iii)   Invite God into your heart, your mind, your spirit and your body; asking that you might love God 'with all your heart, and with all your soul, and with all your mind, and with all your strength' (Mark 12:30).

(iv)   Read your chosen text through meditatively, pausing as often as you need to let words and images resonate within you. Ponder whether there are ways that this text brings to mind your own relationship with God. Allow yourself to recognize also places of discomfort and dissonance in your encounter with the text.

(v)   Offer to God your feelings and reflections.

(vi)   Ask that God may continue to reveal Godself to you in ways that draw you to the divine with love and longing.

(vii)   Close by saying the Lord's Prayer, either in the traditional form or in these words by Canadian Anglican Frances Somerville: 'Yabban Yamman, Timeless and loving, creator of all, Your name is holy. We seek to do your will that your purpose may prevail. We ask you for the bread of life and for the power to forgive. For all your gifts and constant love your holy name be blest and praised, now and forever. Yabban, Yamman. Amen.'

Questions for further reflection

(1)   Mechthild of Magdeburg's sensual imagery is not to everyone's taste, some readers finding it overblown and feeling that it arises out of the repression of natural sexual experiences. Do you think that it is a healthy expression of spirituality? Would it be conceivable for a man to have such an eroticized concept of union with God?

(2)   Ignatian spirituality takes desire very seriously and sees it as one of the primary routes into a deeper relationship with God. In order for this to be so it also believes that when individuals uncover their true desires these will be found to focus on the love of God and on service in God's world. Is this credible from

your understanding of human nature? Does it reflect a theology which does not take seriously enough the effect of the Fall on humanity, or is it true to our nature as beings created in God's image?

(3) Female imagery of God still causes controversy within the Church. Do you think it should be an integral part of Christian spirituality, or do female images detract from Christian understandings of who God is?

Notes

1. The Flowing Light of the Godhead, Book II, Chapter 26 in Mechthild of Magdeburg: The Flowing Light of the Godhead, ed. Frank Tobin, New Jersey: Paulist Press, 1998, p.97.
2. The Flowing Light of the Godhead, Book VI, Chapter 1.
3. The Flowing Light of the Godhead, Book I, Chapter 44.
4. Though this is something that she does subvert right at the beginning of her book when God is heralded as the elusive and superior Lady Love by the male troubadour soul languishing in love for her, in conscious parody of contemporary court poetry.
5. The Flowing Light of the Godhead, Book VI, Chapter 21.
6. The Flowing Light of the Godhead, Book IV, Chapter 19.
7. Frederick Buechner, Wishful Thinking: A Seeker's ABC, San Francisco: Harper and Row, 1973, p.119.
8. Janet Morley, London: SPCK, 1988.
9. Janet Morley, All Desires Known, London: SPCK, 1988, pp.91–2.
10. Not that female images for God cannot be found in earlier sources: there are, for example, maternal images of God in the Bible as well as a long tradition in which Wisdom – God's spirit at action in the world – is personified as female. However it is only in recent years that such images and language are finding an accepted place within Christian public worship.
11. All Desires Known, p.94.
12. Edwina Gateley: A Warm Moist Salty God: Women Journeying Towards Wisdom, Trabuco Canyon: Source Books, 1993, p.90.

Chapter 7

Mystery

I know a person in Christ who fourteen years ago was caught up to the third heaven – whether in the body or out of the body I do not know; God knows. And I know that such a person – whether in the body or out of the body I do not know; God knows – was caught up into Paradise and heard things that are not to be told, that no mortal is permitted to repeat.

2 Corinthians 12:2–4

I have purposely titled this chapter 'Mystery' rather than 'Mysticism' in order to try to avoid some of the knee-jerk reactions that many people have to that word. For some it conjures up the idea of a spiritual elite whose ranks they can never hope to enter: a cadre of experts in prayer who are especially beloved by God and uniquely close to God. For others, it is a word which speaks not of an elite to be aspired to but of balderdash and nonsense – a disembodied spirituality of no use either for one's real life in the world of hard facts or for the hard work of building up the reign of God in the world as it really is. However 'mystery' may be a more open term, reminding us that however far we are along our path to God there is always more to discover and to delight us: an invitation to continue the journey and always to be ready to be surprised at what God chooses to reveal to us and where following in Christ's footsteps may take us.

So with that as our overarching framework for a chapter dealing with mystery, we can look at some of the definitions of mysticism with the expectation of finding them challenging but not exclusive, God-oriented but also concerned with the wellbeing of this world. Evelyn Underhill, the English author of some of the best explanatory work on Mysticism in the twentieth century, defines it this way: 'Mysticism is the art of union with Reality. The mystic is a person who has attained that union in greater or lesser degree; or who aims at and believes in such attainment.'[1] This definition is intended to cover mysticism across religious boundaries rather than referring to Christian mysticism exclusively: hence the use of the word 'Reality' when a theist religion would be more likely to use 'God'. Its main usefulness is in introducing the theme of union, which is at the heart of mystic prayer, and also of presenting the idea that mysticism, rather than taking one out of the real world, takes one into the realm of truth and out of that of our daily illusions. A recurring theme within mystic writings across religions is that it is only through union with the source of all being that we properly understand both ourselves and also the reality that surrounds us.

But this definition is insufficient to introduce us to Christian mysticism which, while sharing universal themes of union and the banishment of illusion, has certain characteristics which belong to it alone. These come from our understanding of the nature of God, and the way that God relates to humanity and the world. In particular the movement of the incarnation, which shows us a God who invites us to follow this direction into the middle of human mess and crisis rather than seeking to escape from it in blissful union with a divinity that is detached from human suffering. Rowan Williams sees such a movement into the world as well as into the divine as the one characteristic that we can use to discern a true Christian mystic, the way that we can identify that God has brought to birth within them a true likeness to the divine: 'If the "mystical" ultimately means the reception of a particular *pattern* of divine action (creative love, self-emptying incarnation), its test will be the presence or absence of something like that pattern in a human life seen as a whole, not the presence or absence of this or that phenomenon in the consciousness.'[2] Mysticism is not about seeing visions and dreaming dreams, it is about becoming more like God in our attitude to and actions in the world that is both God's and ours.

So the mystery we find on our spiritual journey is not primarily to do with coming to an experience of an altered state of consciousness, and definitely nothing to do with being a favourite of God – true mystics would spurn the message of the fridge magnet I recently saw which said 'Jesus loves you – but I'm his favourite'. It is to do with being caught up into a way of seeing reality that looks for ultimate purpose and meaning rather than being content with surface appearances. It is to do with becoming closer in our relationship with God, and so becoming more open to the needs and wants of all God's children, and, in the process, finding out who we truly are. Our guides into the world of Christian mysticism are three very different characters: Teresa of Avila, a Spanish nun of the sixteenth century; Julian of Norwich, an English lay woman of the thirteenth century; and Etty Hillesum, a Dutch Jew who died at Nazi hands in the Second World War.

Teresa of Avila

Teresa of Avila is one of the best known of the Christian mystics, and the first woman to have been recognized as a Doctor of the Church (a person who has contributed in an outstanding way to our understanding of God and of Christian life) almost 400 years after her death.[3] She was born in 1515, one of twelve children, and entered a Carmelite convent at age twenty. Her first years as a nun were marked by severe illness, bringing her close to death and leaving her paralysed for about three years. Illness continued to plague her throughout her life but, despite this, she managed to found fourteen monasteries of Discalced Carmelites. Discalced literally means 'without shoes' as her nuns wore sandals as a sign of humility; they also followed a stricter and more egalitarian rule than the regular Carmelites and lived in smaller foundations where there was the possibility of mutual support and friendship among all the sisters. Teresa died in 1582, a controversial figure both for her reforming zeal, which brought her into conflict with some members of her order, and for her writings which received both admiration and also a certain amount of suspicion from Church authorities.

Teresa wrote in her native Spanish and has left two explorations of prayer and the life of the spirit: *The Way of Perfection* and, considered her masterpiece by many, *The Interior Castle*, as well as an autobiography, *The Book of Her Life*, a later account of her monastic foundations, *The Book of Her Foundations*, and *Meditation on the Song of Songs*. Her own spiritual life was marked by a number of 'supernatural' phenomena: what she called locutions – hearing the voice of God or Christ speaking directly to her soul, intellectual visions – experiences of the presence of Christ beside her and imaginative visions – the appearance of the divine persons to the inner being. However, she did not see these as the end point of a spiritual life but as consolations and helps on the way to becoming Christlike, as she says in *The Interior Castle*. 'His Majesty [God] couldn't grant us a greater favour than to give us a life that would be an imitation of the life His beloved Son lived.'[4]

In Teresa's understanding, the life of prayer moves ideally from being something that we do to becoming something that God does in us. One of her most famous ways of illustrating this comes from *The Way of Perfection* and is based on the image of the soul as a garden that needs the water of prayer in order to both survive and flourish. At first the only way to get this water to it is to draw it by hand from the well, something which takes a lot of effort on the individual's part. As the person gets more accustomed to spending time in the recollection of God's presence the watering comes as if from a water-wheel or aqueduct, in other words, with less effort on their part. However, at this stage they are still doing the work themselves. In the next stage God begins to be the one who is more active: providing water from a river or stream which the person merely needs to direct into the soul; while in the fourth stage God rains down water freely on the garden as free gift with no work on the individual's part whatsoever. Teresa's imagery is often more evocative than it is clearly articulated, but her main message seems to be that, as the soul becomes more open to God, God delights in choosing to work within and give us more insight and sense of union than our own efforts could ever hope to achieve.

In Teresa's most complete work on the life of prayer, the image of a garden is replaced by that of a castle, which she takes as a basis for beginning her writing: 'It is that we consider our soul to be like a castle made entirely out of a diamond or of very clear crystal, in which there are many rooms, just as in heaven there are many dwelling places.'[5] *The Interior Castle* then takes the reader on a guided tour of this delightful residence, drawing ever closer to its centre, in which sits the King, God, whose light is shed throughout the castle though to different degrees. It is worth noting that the soul for Teresa is a site of great beauty, and the natural dwelling place for God. Despite the fact that malevolent creatures dwell in the moat outside and attack it – these being our sins and the devils that made up part of her understanding of the universe – it is a place of delight and a fit home for the divine.

Teresa encourages her readers to roam through the castle, moving from its outer edges into its God-filled interior. In the same way as with the image of watering the garden, the further you penetrate into the castle the less progress depends on the pray-er and the more it rests on God's gracious gift. In Teresa's opinion not all Christians will make it very far inside: only those who are willing to suffer and give up much for their God, and who persist in living a holy and prayerful life, are likely to find the innermost dwelling places – and, even then, this can never be earned but is always at the good grace of God to give or withhold as is best for each individual soul. In the seventh dwelling place, the very heart of the castle, it is as if the soul is married to God in a union which cannot be broken and which makes them one, though still distinct as is the case with married couples in Teresa's understanding: 'For He has desired to be so joined with the creature, that, just as those who are married cannot be separated, He doesn't want to be separated from the soul.'[6]

This union is still not an end in itself but the starting place for a life more open to service in the world: 'the purpose of this spiritual marriage: the birth always of good works, good works.'[7] Teresa brings together the different vocations of Mary and Martha, the contemplative and the worker, believing that it is possible for the innermost soul to remain in communion with God while the mind and body are both busy doing the Lord's business. And the business that we do doesn't have to be great and heroic, it is more important that, however small it may be, it is undertaken and accomplished with love.[8]

Although Teresa does not believe that all Christians have a calling from God that will carry them into the seventh dwelling place, there is one room that she thinks everyone must frequently re-visit, whether they are in the innermost or outermost rooms. This is the room of self-awareness where we learn who we truly are in humility and with candid gaze. Such self knowledge is the opposite of either navel-gazing self-fascination or of false and grovelling humility: it is the basis for opening ourselves to God with honesty and trust. For Teresa we cannot know ourselves without also growing in knowledge of God, and learning more about ourselves will not lead to self-obsession but to a turning towards the God who created and loves us and is far more than we will ever dream of being.

Teresa's mysticism is one that begins in self-knowledge, that leads to service, that is explored in friendship and that is always companioned by Jesus Christ. Unlike some other mystic writers she never wanted people to become detached from their human relationships, as she says about her new monastic foundations: 'all must be friends, all must be loved, all must be held dear, and all must be helped.'[9] Neither did she want them to leave behind the companionship and model of the life of Jesus, saying: 'Jesus is too good a companion for us to turn away from him and his most beloved mother.'[10] The mystery that Teresa leads us to explore is at the same time divine and obscure as it is human and grounded in incarnation and service. Hers is a distinctively Christian mysticism which is of continuing value to read and explore today.

Exercise 7.1: Friendship with God

Teresa said of prayer in *The Book of Her Life*: 'mental prayer … is nothing else than an intimate sharing between friends; it means taking time frequently to be alone with Him who we know loves us.' Take time over the course of a fortnight to be with God in friendship. You might structure this around quiet time at home, by taking time to walk with God as your companion, or by inviting God to be with you when you are doing anything that you enjoy – as you might with one of your friends.

Teresa also said of prayer that: 'it is in the effects and deeds following afterwards that one discerns the true value of prayer.' Take time also over the course of a fortnight to find a way of serving others of God's friends. This could be by doing someone else's chores, by getting in touch with someone you know is lonely, by speaking up for a person or group you see being belittled, or by any other sign of friendship that feels authentic to you.

Julian of Norwich

Our second guide into mystery lived three hundred years before Teresa in the east of England. We don't know her birth name, only the one that was given to her from the name of the church where she lived: St Julian's in Norwich. She seems, from the level of literacy she shows, to have come from a family of some standing into which she was born in December 1342. She lived through a time of great social and political turmoil, with the Black Death having killed about a third of the entire population, leaving no family untouched and social and political turmoil in its wake. In fact Julian's local bishop spent more time as a war lord suppressing peasant unrest than as a spiritual leader. During these tumultuous years she discovered a vocation as an anchorite and was the first-ever woman to write a book in English: her wonderful *Revelations of Divine Love* (also translated into modern English as *Showings of Divine Love*).

Before looking at her writing it's worth exploring what it meant to be an anchorite – not a very familiar religious term. Anchorites were individuals, most often women, who lived a particular version of the eremitic life. On taking their vows they took up residence in a cell attached to a church, which had one window looking on to the street and one looking in to the church. The liturgy at their entry included parts of the funeral service to remind them that this room was to be their grave and that they were never to leave it again. However, they were not totally isolated. They often had a maid to look after their daily needs and they used the window to the world to offer spiritual counsel and comfort to any who sought them out. In the English rule for anchorites, the *Ancrene Wisse* written in the late twelfth century, there were instructions for the organizing of their spiritual lives and also of their outer lives; including advice against keeping cows, which might cause neighbourly friction by running amok, but permitting the keeping of a cat.

Julian's theology and spiritual understanding was centred on a series of visions that she had on 8 May 1373, at the age of 30. She describes how she had prayed for an illness which would bring her closer to God (a strange concept to us today but one which reflected the spiritual honour associated with suffering in her time), and it was at the moment when her life was despaired of that she saw a vision of Christ on the cross. Her conversations with this visionary Christ provided the material for years of thought and meditation, eventually becoming the longer version of her *Revelations*. She always believed that the vision was not for her benefit alone but was to be shared with other members of Christ's Church: people she called 'even-Christians', meaning by this the ordinary members of the church living out their faith in ordinary ways amid the demands of ordinary lives.

Julian wants to share with these even-Christians the understanding of God that had come to her from her visions themselves
and from her reflections on them over the years. She is not interested
in inciting others to experience the sort of illness and subsequent
mystical experience that she went through but to enable them to
better understand the true nature of God and the way that God
relates to his beloved creatures. This is the way that she describes the
God she encountered:

> His demeanour was merciful, his face was a lovely pale brown
> with a very seemly countenance, his eyes were black, most
> beautiful and seemly, revealing all his loving pity, and within
> him there was a secure place of refuge, long and broad, all full
> of heavenliness. And the loving regard which he kept on his
> servant (that is all humanity), and especially when he fell, it
> seemed to me that it could melt our hearts for love and break
> them in two for joy. This lovely regard had in it a beautiful
> mingling which was wonderful to see. Part was compassion
> and pity, part was joy and bliss. The joy and bliss surpass the
> compassion and pity, as far as heaven is above earth.[11]

Julian's image of the servant is how she pictures sinning humanity.
What is particular to herself about her vision is that there is no
anger in God towards this servant, merely love and compassion. The
mystery of God that Julian discovers is that the anger we fear is not
present in him – there is nothing in God to frighten us, all that God
offers to us is gentle encouragement and delight in our seeking of him.

One way that Julian uses to explain this nature of God is to look to
maternal imagery:

> This fair lovely word 'mother' is so sweet and so kind in itself
> that it cannot be truly said of anyone or to anyone except of him
> and to him who is the true mother of life and of all things. To
> the property of motherhood belong nature, love, wisdom and

knowledge, and this is God ... The kind, loving mother who knows and sees the need of her child guards it very tenderly, as the nature and condition of motherhood will have. And always as the child grows in age and in stature, she acts differently, but she does not change her love.[12]

This beautiful passage says much about Julian's view of God, and also about her understanding of the spiritual life. God is tender and wise, always reaching out in love to her child. Part of God's wisdom is to know that our relationship with her will change as our spiritual journey progresses, or sometimes meanders, along. We can know that God will always be with us, but we can also expect that this loving presence will be experienced differently at different times, reflecting ways that we have changed and grown in our human and spiritual maturity. It can also be a gift to us, as explored in the last chapter, to have imagery of God which breaks out of the usual male mold and allows us to say with Julian, 'as truly as God is our Father, so truly is God our mother'.[13]

Julian's view of the nature of God led her to have a very hopeful view of life, expressed in her most famous saying: 'All shall be well, and all shall be well, and all manner of things shall be well.'[14] This may sound a tad glib to some ears, and Julian herself found it difficult to understand how this could be, questioning God further about it. She then says: 'But I had no answer to this revelation save this: 'What is impossible to you is not impossible to me. I shall honour my word in every respect, and I will make everything turn out for the best.' Her hope depends on her understanding of who God is: the loving father and mother who takes delight in his child and wants only what is best for it. Her visions and revelations do not show her details of God's plans for humanity, only that the motive and intention behind all of them is always perfect love, as she says in her final chapter:

So it was that I learned that love was our Lord's meaning. And I saw for certain, both here and elsewhere, that before ever he made us, God loved us; and that his love has never slackened, nor ever shall. In this love all his works have been done, and in this love he has made everything serve us; and in this love our life is everlasting. Our beginning was when we were made, but the love in which he made us never has beginning. In it we have our beginning.[15]

Julian invites us into the mystery of a God who loves us, even when we are at our most undeserving. She doesn't dictate a particular spiritual path, but rather helps make possible a particular spiritual demeanour by emphasizing the welcome that God always has for us – a demeanour of gratitude, of hope and of reciprocal love for the one who loves us so generously. This is available to all her even-Christians who will never see visions or spend their lives in the discipline of an anchor-hold. Julian was a woman who spent most of her life in a small room with one window looking into the church and one into the world but, despite or because of this physical restriction, she was able both to see and to share truths of profound and lasting significance about the God whom we seek on whatever Christian spiritual path we follow.

Exercise 7.2: The loving gaze of God

Julian invites us to gaze into the loving eyes of God and one way we can do this is through using icons in our prayer. Icons are traditionally known as windows into the divine – images which show us something of the divine nature and invite us to contemplate it. This is what Julian found in her visions, but, for most of us, we benefit from a physical object to focus our gaze on.

(i)   Find an icon image that you are drawn to. There are many books containing icons, as well as a number of images on-line. For this exercise look particularly for images of Christ or of the Trinity. If you are comfortable with the idea you might also use an icon of the Blessed Virgin Mary as a window into the motherhood of God.

(ii)   Find a place where you can comfortably contemplate the image, and begin your time of prayer by inviting God to reveal something of the divine nature of love through your contemplation.

(iii)   Sit quietly with the icon, letting your eyes rest lovingly on it and allowing it to speak to you in whatever way you can receive. Stay with the image that first drew you even if you are not quite sure what it represents for you.

(iv)   Bring to mind Julian's words about the loving gaze of God resting on all creation and become conscious, as far as you are able, of God's eyes gazing at you with this unconditional love.

(v)   Give thanks to God for the gift of sight, for the gift of the icon writer (icons are 'written' rather than 'painted' because they are primarily acts of prayer rather than of creativity), and, most of all, for the love which God has for you.

(vi)   Close with the words of this collect for Julian of Norwich: 'Loving God, in your compassion you granted to the Lady Julian many revelations of your nurturing and sustaining love: Move our hearts, like hers, to seek you above all things, for in giving us yourself you give us all; through Jesus Christ our Lord, who lives and reigns with you and the Holy Spirit, one God, for ever and ever. Amen.'

An interrupted life

Many mystics could claim to live interrupted lives – ones which are knocked off their intended conventional course by the action of God within them. Our third guide into the mystery of God had an interrupted life in a far more tragic way: she was killed in Auschwitz on 30 November 1943 at the age of 29. Her name is Etty Hillesum and she was a Dutch Jew who lived in Amsterdam until her life was caught up in the Nazi persecution. She was not a practising Jew, and neither did she describe herself as a Christian, though she did happily accept the label 'Christian' when a friend applied it to her understanding of life,[16] and she certainly experienced God in a way which echoes that of earlier Christian mystics. This experience she speaks of in moving words which are maybe more accessible than some of the traditional mystic writings. Her thoughts come down to us in a diary she kept for the last two years of her life; a document which reflects the outward reality of life in the occupied Netherlands and also which is very frank about the inward reality of Etty's own being.

At the beginning of Etty's diary she is involved intellectually, emotionally and sexually with an older man, Julius Spier, who was the charismatic founder of 'psychochirology' – the dubious art or science of reading people's characters from their palm prints. Etty seems to have been drawn to him both by sexual attraction and also because she was beginning to seek for a deeper reality in her own life, to which he seemed to offer a gateway. At this stage she is not an altogether attractive character. There is a sense that her self-scrutiny is close to self-absorption, particularly in the way that she is seemingly able to pay little attention to the effects the Nazi occupation is having both on her city and particularly on the Jews. However, she wrestles with her own tendency to grandiosity with honesty and an awareness that she may not be unique in her inner complexity, saying to herself: 'Don't overestimate your own intensity; it may give you the impression that you are cut out for greater things than the so-called man in the street, whose inner life is a closed book to you.'[17]

Etty early on also understands that her inward quest cannot be a total end in itself; that she needs to engage with the reality outside herself as well as with the reality within if she is to develop into the fully alive human being that she seeks to become.

This means that her exploration of the mystery of herself and of God needs to take place in the midst of her current reality rather than in retreat from the world to a place of especial security and sanctity. Like many of us she is aware of a longing within herself to find just such a place, but is prepared to fight against it in order to achieve greater integrity between her inner and outer life:

Sometimes I long for a convent cell, with the sublime wisdom of centuries set out on bookshelves all along the wall and a view across the cornfields – there must be cornfields and they must wave in the breeze – and there I would immerse myself in the wisdom of ages and in myself. Then I might perhaps find peace and clarity. But that would be no great feat. It is right here, in this very place, in the here and now, that I must find them.[18]

It is always tempting to quote Etty at length because she writes with passion and clarity about the truths that she is discovering, and the excitement that accompanies such inner travels. She is a clearly fallible young woman whose honesty about her own failings makes her easier for many of us to identify with and so to believe that some of her discoveries might also become our own.

One way that Etty talks about herself is as a girl who learnt how to kneel, or how to pray: 'What a strange story it really is, my story: the girl who could not kneel. Or its variation: the girl who learned to pray.'[19] Along the way of learning this new possibility she also discovered, like Julian, a very distinct vision of who God is and the relationship of the divine with the world and with herself. And this God is not somewhere 'out there' but somewhere deep within: not so much a lover calling to the beloved, but one that we find within our own deepest selves dwelling, as Teresa also found, deep at the heart of our being, waiting for us to come to him there: 'There is a really deep well inside me. And in it dwells God. Sometimes I am there too. But more often stones and grit block the well, and God is buried beneath. Then He must be dug out again.'[20] God is not to be identified with the human person – Etty never loses an awareness that God is much more than a truth within herself – but God is to be found through the inner quest: this is the route into the divine mystery that she finds and shares with us.

It should be no surprise, however, that this inner journey also involves an outer journey. The God that Etty discovers within is not a secret, comforting reality for herself alone but calls for and enables engagement with others:

Truly my life is one long hearkening unto my self and unto others, unto God. And if I say that I hearken, it is really God who hearkens inside me. The most essential and the deepest in me hearkening unto the most essential and deepest in the other. God to God.[21]

This becomes apparent as her diary continues, with the focus becoming far less on her spiritual explorations alone and including much more consideration of the brutal events unfolding around her. She becomes increasingly aware of her place within a community of people who share her growing feelings of daily worry, fear and sick-heartedness; and also increasingly aware of a call within her to help this community:

This much I know: you have to forget your own worries for the sake of others, for the sake of those whom you love. All the strength and love and faith in God which one possesses, and which have grown so miraculously in me of late, must be there for everyone who chances to cross one's path and who needs it.[22]

The somewhat self-obsessed young woman who began the diary has made the classic journey within Christian mysticism from a personal and intimate encounter with God to an opening up to the needs of all God's children in imitation of the love that has been found within.

This love took Etty to work in Westerbork, the transit camp for Jews from Amsterdam from which the trains left for Aushwitz and death. It was Etty's hope that she could bring God with her into this place of pain and fear, and become 'the thinking heart of the barracks': a presence of love and concern for others, with a practical eye for what could help to ease their circumstances. In this work she did not lose all concern for herself and for her family, but continued to live into a love which took the needs of all as equally important; the last words of her diary are 'We should be willing to act as a balm for all wounds'.[23] Through all of this she still managed to see herself as held safe within God's arms, and somehow free of the Nazi's clutches even though they had control over her body and outer self.

The God in whose arms she was held seemed to Etty to be a God of vulnerability rather than of power: she did not hold God responsible for the cruelty of the times, nor did she believe that God could intervene to save humanity from itself. Instead it was our job to protect God: 'You cannot help us but we must help You and defend Your dwelling place inside us to the last.'[24] The mystery of God for Etty was not the uncovering of power and glory but the discovery of the way that he entrusted himself to us, and entrusted us to one another. The help that God could give did not lie in changing circum stances and providing rescue, but in suffering with us and alerting us to the love that should be the bedrock of all human relations.

Etty's spiritual path was formed by this understanding: leading her to stand, with God, in the midst of suffering rather than to try to escape from it; strengthened to do so by her awareness of God's companionship deep within her and by her paradoxical insight that it was up to her to protect God rather than the other way around. She was able to access deep inner joy in the midst of almost indescribable suffering, as she explains in a letter written on 18 August 1943 less than a month before her final journey to Auschwitz:

> You have made me so rich, Oh God, please let me share out Your beauty with open hands. My life has become an uninterrupted dialogue with You, oh God, one great dialogue. Sometimes when I stand in some corner of the camp, my feet planted on Your earth, my eyes raised towards Your Heaven, tears sometimes run down my face, tears of deep emotion and gratitude.[25]

Etty, the mystic who found out how to pray, how to serve and how to love, was taken from Westerbork on 7 September 1943 and died in Auschwitz just over two months later.

Exercise 7.3: Praying with Etty

'Ultimately, we have just one moral duty: to reclaim large areas of peace in ourselves, more and more peace and to reflect it towards others. And the more peace there is in us, the more peace there will also be in our troubled world.'[26]

(i)   Each morning for a week commit yourself to getting up 10 minutes earlier than you would normally need to.

(ii)   Find a peaceful place to spend this extra 10 minutes: this could even be still in bed as long as you are able to resist falling back to sleep.

(iii)   Begin your 10 minutes by asking God to grant you the grace of peace within yourself in this new day.

(iv)   Then think through the up-coming day and identify times or encounters which might shake your inner peace.

(v)   Open these up to God, asking for especial grace to allow you to pass through these times and encounters with continuing peace.

(vi)   Continue by asking God that this peace may be a deep well within you that not only refreshes you but which spills out to touch all those who are part of your life this day.

(vii)   Close with these words, or any other similar prayer that comes naturally to you: 'May the peace of God, which passes all understanding, fill my heart, my mind, my body and my soul this day that I may be a source of God's peace for my family, my friends, my community and all this troubled world. Amen.'

Questions for further reflection

(1) Teresa of Avila is very clear that final mystical union with God can only come as free gift and cannot be achieved through our own efforts in prayer. She is less clear about why this gift is offered to some but not all, her only explanation being that it is not for the benefit of all souls to receive it. Does Teresa's

understanding of mystic union gel with your theological understanding of the nature of God? Is it loving of God to instill a longing for union with the divine which God chooses not to fulfil?

(2) Julian of Norwich is as much a theologian as a writer of spirituality, and central to her theology is an understanding of God as being without anger. This contradicts some interpretations of biblical teaching, though by no means all. Do you think Julian was re-making God in her own image, or was she entrusted with a true theological insight?

(3) Etty Hillesum never called herself a Christian, even though she did accept that title for her unfolding spirituality and worldview. Do you think that it is proper to include her in a book focused on Christian spirituality?

Notes

1. Evelyn Underhill, *Practical Mysticism: A Little Book for Normal People*, Guildford: Eagle, 1991 (first published 1914), p.2.
2. Rowan Williams, *Teresa of Avila*, London: Geoffrey Chapman, 1991, pp.145–6.
3. By Pope Paul VI on 27 September 1970.
4. *The Interior Castle*, 7:4,4 in the translation by Kieran Kavanaugh, OCD, and Otilio Rodriguez, OCD, New York: Paulist Press, 1979, p.189. All quotations from *The Interior Castle* are from this edition.
5. *The Interior Castle*, 1:1,1, p.35.
6. *The Interior Castle*, 7:2,3, p.178.
7. *The Interior Castle*, 7:4,6, p.190.
8. *The Interior Castle*, 7:4,16, p.194.
9. *The Way of Perfection*, 4:7, quoted in Rowan Williams, *Teresa of Avila*, London: Geoffrey Chapman, 1991, p.81.
10. Quoted by Rowan Williams, *Teresa of Avila*, 1991, p.133.
11. Julian of Norwich, *Showings*, Chapter 51, in the *Classics of Western Spirituality* series, *Julian*, eds. Edmund Colledge and James Walsh, New York: Paulist Press, 1978, p.271.
12. *Showings*, Chapter 60, as above, pp.298–9.
13. *Showings*, Chapter 59, as above, p.295.
14. *Showings*, Chapter 31, as above, p.229.
15. *Revelations of Divine Love*, Chapter 33, tr. Clifton Wolters, Middlesex: Penguin, 1966, p.212.
16. See *An Interrupted Life: The Diaries of Etty Hillesum 1941–43*, tr. A. J. Pomerans, intro. J. G. Gaarlandt, New York: Washington Square Press, 1985, pp.222–3.

17. Monday 10 March 1941 from *An Interrupted Life*, p.8.
18. *An Interrupted Life*, p.36.
19. *An Interrupted Life*, p.240.
20. *An Interrupted Life*, p.44.
21. *An Interrupted Life*, p.214.
22. *An Interrupted Life*, p.175.
23. *An Interrupted Life*, p.243.
24. *An Interrupted Life*, p.187.
25. *An Interrupted Life*, p.255.
26. *An Interrupted Life*, p.229.

Benediction

It seems inappropriate to end a book on the spiritual life with a conclusion: our spiritual journeying into the mystery of this God who is far beyond our comprehension yet always calling to us in love never reaches a conclusion, at least this side of the grave. There is always more to discover – more love to experience, more activity to be called into, more fellowship to share, more silence to open up within ourselves. The infinite source of love and truth has chosen to be open to our finite selves and to offer us more than we could ever ask or imagine. This offering is made to all God's children, all the multitude of women and men who bear God's image, are in-dwelt by God's Spirit and who are the beloved sisters and brothers of the incarnate Christ. Which means that this spiritual journeying is not for a set-apart breed of super-Christians but for all of us who feel drawn to God – all of us who want to learn more about who God is and who we are, and who feel a need to explore beneath the surface appearance of things to find a deeper and more meaningful reality.

One of the best helps for the continuing journey is to make it in company, more especially in the company of one who is a spiritual companion or director. Like any exploration our spiritual journey may take us into places that we didn't expect to be and which we find confusing or even overwhelming. At these times having a guide who has walked this path before, or has spent time with others on this journey – whether in person or in their writings – can be an invaluable aid. They can look with us at what God is doing in our lives: at where we are with God at this present moment and where we might be being called to go next. They can temper our enthusiasm with wisdom, remind us that wilderness experiences are not uncommon or necessarily barren, and, more prosaically, suggest new ways that we can pray and new books that we might read.

A spiritual director, despite the title, is not there to direct our journey with God, but to help us discover it for ourselves. They are not in any way between us and God, but by our side providing companionship and, most importantly, a listening ear attentive to our silences as well as to our speech. They are not just for 'professional Christians' – clergy and members of religious orders – but for anyone who is interested in committing themselves to deepening their spiritual life. As with any relationship, not every spiritual director is right for every individual so it is important to put some thought and care into finding someone who is right for you. A common starting point is to speak to a priest or minister in a local congregation and find out if they have contacts in this field: a personal recommendation is usually more trustworthy than looking for someone on the web.

Although this book has only sampled some of the resources and riches of the Christian tradition, I hope it has been able to do one very important thing. That is to make it clear that there is no one right way of prayer, no one spiritual path which is right for all of us all of the time. There are some who are called to the way of silence, and who find in it a wonderful path into union with the divine. There are others who are called to experience and celebrate the presence of God in creation, and who give voice to the goodness and delight inherent in this world and the beauty that surrounds us. Still others find God through being inspired by scriptural teaching into social action on behalf of the marginalized and oppressed, and walk a spiritual way in which the love of neighbour leads them ever deeper into the love of God. And it may be that the same person will walk on different paths at different times, finding a way of prayer that helps them for a while but which may need to be changed as their life and circumstances alter. The love and generosity of God is seen in God's willingness to allow us to find our own way to the door of the divine, encouraging exploration rather than dictating a single track.

The one fundamental to all our Christian spiritual paths is that the initiative on this journey does not lie with us. We seek God only because God first seeks us. This book's title is taken from a prayer poem by Michael Leunig, which is printed in full at the front, and which talks of the flowers, the thorns, the dreams and the strangeness of the paths which lead us to God's door. But while we experience the path as our walk towards God, the door has actually already been opened and God has trod the path towards us before ever we began the journey towards God. It is not up to us to find God, it is rather up to us to open ourselves so that we can realize the truth that God has already found us, and already holds us close to the divine heart. The different paths of prayer are just different ways for allowing this opening to happen, windows into the greater reality which is the true ground of our being, source of our love, and the end of our longing.

So journey well, and take with you this blessing from the Celtic tradition, knowing always that God, the one who creates us, companions us and dwells within us, will be with you every step of the way:

May God's peace be yours,
And well, and seven times well
May you spend your lives.

May you be an isle in the sea,
May you be a hill on the shore,
May you be a star in the darkness,
May you be a staff to the weak,
May the peace Christ Jesus gave fill every heart for you
May the peace Christ Jesus gave fill you for everyone.
Amen

Glossary

Apophatic theology/spirituality   A way of knowing God that believes we can only talk about what God is not rather than what God is, a way of no names or images for God. Also known as Negative Theology.

Askesis   Greek word meaning training or discipline: the sort of striving an athlete would put into succeeding.

Divinization   The work of God's grace within humanity bringing human beings into closer likeness of and union with God. Also known as theosis or deification.

Eremetical   The way of life of the hermit.

Geordie   A resident of Newcastle upon Tyne. The term is used both by locals and outsiders.

Hesychasm   A mystical tradition of prayer within the Orthodox Church. It may involve particular body postures and breathing control in order to deaden the senses and achieve inner and outer silence.

Impassible   Not subject to pain or any form of emotion. A theological term used to refer to the unchanging nature of God who is not moved or changed by any passions.

Kataphatic theology/spirituality   A way of knowing God that uses an abundance of names and images to talk about God. Also known as Positive or Affirmative Theology.

Koan   A Zen saying or story designed to take the hearer beyond the working of the logical mind.

Mondo   A Zen dialogue between a master and students, often playful.

Praxis   The practical application or practice of a belief system or school of thought. Liberation Theology often stresses ortho-praxis (right action) over orthodoxy (right belief).

Syncretism   Reconciling or fusing divergent systems of belief to make one melded belief system. Often criticized for minimizing the real differences between belief systems.

Suggestions for Further Reading

Ascetic spirituality
Athanasius: The Life of Antony and the Letter To Marcellinus, Robert C. Gregg, New Jersey: Paulist Press, 1979. Athanasius' life of Antony is one of the classical texts on ascetic spirituality. Understanding it may be helped by reading David Brakke's book *Athanasius and Asceticism* (The John Hopkins University Press, 1997) though this does focus on Church history and theology rather than spirituality.

Body prayer
Prayer and Our Bodies, Flora Slosson Wuellner, Nashville: The Upper Room, 1998. A very useful look at bodily prayer and the healing it may offer. Wuellner integrates the physical and the spiritual so that our whole selves may be brought into our prayer lives.

Celtic spirituality
The Celtic Way of Prayer, Second Edition, Esther de Waal, London: Hodder and Stoughton, 2003 (1996). A deeply grounded exploration of the riches of the Celtic tradition which includes many Celtic poems, prayers and stories. Esther de Waal's experience as a leader of retreats comes through in the way that she makes the material speak to contemporary needs.

Anam Cara: A Book of Celtic Wisdom, John O'Donohue, New York: Harper Collins, 1998. A contemporary take on spirituality strongly rooted in the Celtic tradition. 'Anam cara' means 'soul friend' and this book explores ways in which we are befriended on our journey to explore and live out our true humanity.

Prayer books from the Iona Community. There are a number of books which contain liturgical material – poetry, hymns, service outlines – from the ecumenical Iona Community which integrates Celtic spirituality with a focus on justice and peace work in contemporary society. They are a great resource for personal and public prayer.

Centering prayer
Open Mind, Open Heart: The Contemplative Dimension of the Gospels, Thomas Keating, New York: Continuum, 1994. This is the classic introduction to the modern movement of centering prayer which looks both at its history within Christianity and also gives a detailed introduction to its practice.

Centering Prayer and Inner Awakening, Cynthia Bourgeault, Cambridge, MA: Cowley Publications, 2004. An introduction from the other main name in the centering prayer movement which is a passionate presentation of the benefits of centering prayer.

The Cloud of Unknowing
The Cloud of Unknowing, ed. James Walsh, S.J., New York: Paulist Press, 1981. This edition includes the complete text of this engaging work along with a useful preface by Simon Tugwell.

Desert Fathers and Mothers
In the Heart of the Desert: The Spirituality of the Desert Fathers and Mothers, John Chryssavgis, Bloomington: World Wisdom, 2003. An excellent thematic approach to the Desert Fathers and Mothers which quotes extensively from the original sources.

The Sayings of the Desert Fathers: The Alphabetical Collection, tr. Benedicta Ward, Kalamazoo: Cistercian Publications, 1975. An excellent translation of the original sayings providing a reasonably comprehensive collection of desert wisdom.

Silence and Honey Cakes: The Wisdom of the Desert, Rowan Williams, Oxford: Lion, 2003. Williams introduces the wisdom of the Desert Fathers and Mothers and looks at how it may continue to resonate within our own spiritual lives. It is an engaging and very readable book.

Eckhart

Meister Eckhart: The Essential Sermons, Commentaries, Treatises and Defense, tr. and intro Edmund Colledge and Bernard McGinn, Paulist Press: New York, 1981. A good selection of Eckhart's writings with a useful introduction to his theology and to the ecclesiastical background to his work.

The Mystical Thought of Meister Eckhart, Bernard McGinn, New York: Crossroad Publishing Company, 2001. A scholarly but still accessible work by one of the leading contemporary experts on Eckhart's thought.

Eco-spirituality

Centuries of Meditations, Thomas Traherne, New York: Cosimo, Inc., 2007 (1908). Thomas Traherne is not, of course, a contemporary writer of eco-spirituality but a seventeenth-century English mystic. I have included this work because it delights in the natural world and breathes a spirit of delight in all creation.

A New Climate for Theology: God, the World, and Global Warming, Sallie McFague, Minneapolis: Fortress Press, 2008. This is a work of theology more than spirituality but it sets out the urgent need for Christians to act on ecological imperatives and to bring their spirituality to bear on the survival of the planet.

Etty Hillesum

An Interrupted Life: The Diaries of Etty Hillesum 1941–43, tr. A. J. Pomerans, intro. J. G. Gaarlandt, New York: Washington Square Press, 1985. The diary really speaks for itself. It is an absorbing read taking you both into the heart of Etty's spiritual growth and into the midst of a heartbreaking period of history.

Eucharistic spirituality

Being as Communion: Studies in the Personhood of the Church, John D. Zizioulas, Crestwood, NY: St. Vladimir's Seminary Press, 1985, reprint 1997. A classic exploration of the meaning of the Eucharist, looking at the role it plays within the life of the Church. Zizioulas writes from the Eastern Orthodox tradition.

The Disabled God: Toward a Liberation Theology of Disability, Nancy L. Eiesland, Nashville: Abingdon Press, 1994. Eiesland writes from a liberation perspective and considers how Eucharistic spirituality should be expressed in a Body of Christ which contains members with disabilities. Those less interested in the development of disability rights activities can skip through some of the earlier chapters.

Feminist imagery

Celebrating Women, eds. Hannah Ward, Jennifer Wild, Janet Morley, Harrisburg: Morehouse, 1995. An eclectic collection of poetry, liturgy, hymns, prayers and psalms showcasing some of the best women's writing in Christian feminist spirituality.

All Desires Known, Janet Morley, Third Edition, Harrisburg: Morehouse, 2006. Janet Morley is one of the most creative voices in providing new liturgical material for both private and public use. This book is a classic, and widely used.

Feminist spirituality

Weaving the Visions: New Patterns in Feminist Spirituality, Carol Christ and Judith Plaskow, New York: HarperOne, 1989. Possibly getting a little dated, but this is still a good place to find the breadth of feminist spirituality – including some which would describe itself as post-Christian or non-Christian.

Heart of Flesh: A Feminist Spirituality for Women and Men, Joan D. Chittister, Grand Rapids: Wm B. Eerdmans Publishing Co., 1998. This is a good introduction to feminist spirituality from one of the leading authors and speakers in the field. Joan Chittister is a Benedictine nun and speaks as one who is committed both to Christianity and to feminism.

Theology by Heart: Women, the Church and God, Ellen Clark-King, Peterborough: Epworth, 2004. This book is a conversation between feminist theology and spirituality and the spiritual experience of working-class women in the north-east of England. It introduces some of the main themes of Christian feminist thought and also the everyday experiences of the divine among a group of 'ordinary' women.

Franciscan spirituality

Celebrating Common Prayer: A Version of the Daily Office SSF, London: Mowbray, 1992. This is a widely loved prayer book which reveals the on-going life of prayer within the Franciscan community. It has orders for prayer offices throughout the day and, while the format can take a little getting to know, it offers great resources for personal and public prayer.

Franciscan Spirituality: Following St Francis Today, Br Ramon, London: SPCK, 1994. This book explores both the history of Franciscan life and its continuing spiritual heritage in the world today. Its author, Br Ramon, is himself an Anglican Franciscan friar and his commitment to, and immersion in, Franciscan spirituality shines through his writing.

Ignatian spirituality

Draw Me Into Your Friendship: A literal translation and a contemporary reading of The Spiritual Exercises, David L. Fleming, Institute of Jesuit Sources, Fifth Edition, 1998. A useful way of presenting the text of Ignatius' Exercises which parallels the original with a modern interpretation.

Inner Compass: An invitation to Ignatian Spirituality, Margaret Silf, Revised Edition, Chicago: Loyola Press, 2007. A clear and excellent introduction to Ignatian spirituality in general and to the Ignatian Exercises in particular.

Sleeping with Bread: Holding What Gives You Life, Dennis Linn, Sheila Fabricant Linn, Matthew Linn, New Jersey: Paulist Press, 1995. A wonderful and very approachable reflection on the Ignatian Examen looking at how it can be used both by individuals and by families.

Jesus Prayer

The Way of a Pilgrim and The Pilgrim Continues His Way, tr. R. M. French, New York: HarperOne, 1991. A nineteenth-century classic of Russian spirituality, written by an anonymous author and telling of his spiritual journey deep into the practice of the Jesus Prayer. It is available in a number of translations, perhaps the best known being by R. M. French in an edition that includes the second volume of this work *The Pilgrim Continues His Way*.

The Jesus Prayer, Simon Barrington-Ward, Abingdon: The Bible Reading Fellowship, 2007 (1996). This is a simple and accessible guide to using the Jesus Prayer in spiritual practice which also gives a little bit of background about its history and roots the prayer in its biblical foundations.

John of the Cross

John of the Cross Selected Writings, ed. Kieran Kavanagh O.C.D., New Jersey: Paulist Press, 1987. A good translation of, and introduction to, John of the Cross's main works. As with all the spiritual classics, there is nothing that beats reading the works as close to the original as it's possible to get.

The Dark Night of the Soul: A Psychiatrist Explores the Connection Between Darkness and Spiritual Growth, Gerald G. May, New York: HarperOne, 2003. More of an exploration of the concept of 'dark night' than of John of the Cross but May builds on John's insights in a way that helps make sense of them to a contemporary readership.

Julian of Norwich

Showings, Julian of Norwich, in the *Classics of Western Spirituality* series, *Julian*, eds. Edmund Colledge and James Walsh, New York: Paulist Press, 1978. A good edition of Julian's writings. It is worth persevering with the occasional inevitable difficulties of a fourteenth-century text for a twenty-first-century reader because the content of Julian's theology and spirituality is richly rewarding.

Julian of Norwich: Mystic and Theologian, Grace Jantzen, London: SPCK, 1987. An excellent introduction to both Julian's spirituality and theology.

Julian: Woman of Our Day, ed. Robert Llewelyn, London: DLT, 1985. A good collection of essays on aspects of Julian's life and writing and their continuing importance in the present day.

Lectio divina
Lectio Divina: Renewing the Ancient Practice of Praying the Scriptures, M. Basil Pennington, New York: Crossroad, 1998. A practical guide to the practice of lectio divina, though the language can be dated and the constant use of 'Lord' may grate on some ears.

Liberation spirituality
We Drink from Our Own Wells: The Spiritual Journey of a People, Gustavo Gutierrez, tr. Matthew J. O'Connell, Maryknoll: Orbis Books Anniversary Edition, 2003 (1983). The classic text of liberation spirituality from the Peruvian theologian who is regarded as one of the founding fathers of Liberation Theology.

Spirituality and Liberation, Robert McAfee Brown, Louisville: The Westminster Press, 1988. A clear and readable exposition of liberation spirituality's rejection of dualism and of the understanding of both spirituality and liberation which results from this approach.

Mechthild of Magdeburg
Mechthild of Magdeburg: The Flowing Light of the Godhead, ed. Frank Tobin, New Jersey: Paulist Press, 1998. This has a useful introduction and a good translation of the text.

Beguine Spirituality: An Anthology, Fiona Bowie, London: SPCK, 1989. This is more of a useful introduction to the Beguines than an anthology, though it does include some extracts from Mechthild, Beatrice of Nazareth and Hadewijch. It helps set Mechthild within her historical context.

Merton, Thomas

New Seeds of Contemplation, Thomas Merton, Boston: Shambhala Publications, 1961. Not an easy read but probably the best introduction to Merton's thinking about the role of contemplation in his life and within Christian spirituality.

Zen and the Birds of Appetite, Thomas Merton, New York: New Directions, 1968. Merton discussing the place of Zen within Christian spirituality.

Living with Wisdom: A Life of Thomas Merton, Jim Forest, Revised Edition, New York: Orbis Books, 2008 (1991). An excellent, readable and honest biography of Merton by Forest who knew Merton personally. It also has many photographs which help make Merton and his surroundings present to the reader.

Mysticism

Mysticism: The Nature and Development of Spiritual Consciousness, Evelyn Underhill, Oxford: Oneworld Publications, 1999 (1911). A classic text on mysticism. If you are daunted by the length (entirely understandably!), try her *Practical Mysticism: A Little Book for Normal People*, Guildford: Eagle, 1991 (1914).

An Anthology of Christian Mysticism, Harvey D. Egan, Second Edition, Collegeville: The Liturgical Press, 1996 (1991). A bit of a tome but useful in bringing together many mystical writings in one volume.

Psalms

Spirituality of the Psalms, Walter Brueggemann, Minneapolis: Augsburg Fortress, 2001. Brueggemann is one of the greatest contemporary experts on praying with the psalms and this book is the abridged, and so more accessible, version of his classic *The Message of the Psalms*. It is especially strong on how the negative psalms can be integrated into spiritual practice.

Teresa of Avila

The Interior Castle, Teresa of Avila, tr. Kieran Kavanaugh, O.C.D. and Otilio Rodriguez, O.C.D., New York: Paulist Press, 1979. There is a good introduction by Kavanaugh which sets the historical and theoretical background for the text that follows.

Teresa of Avila, Rowan Williams, London: Geoffrey Chapman, 1991. An excellent introduction to the thought and spirituality of Teresa.